ALLIE CASAZZA

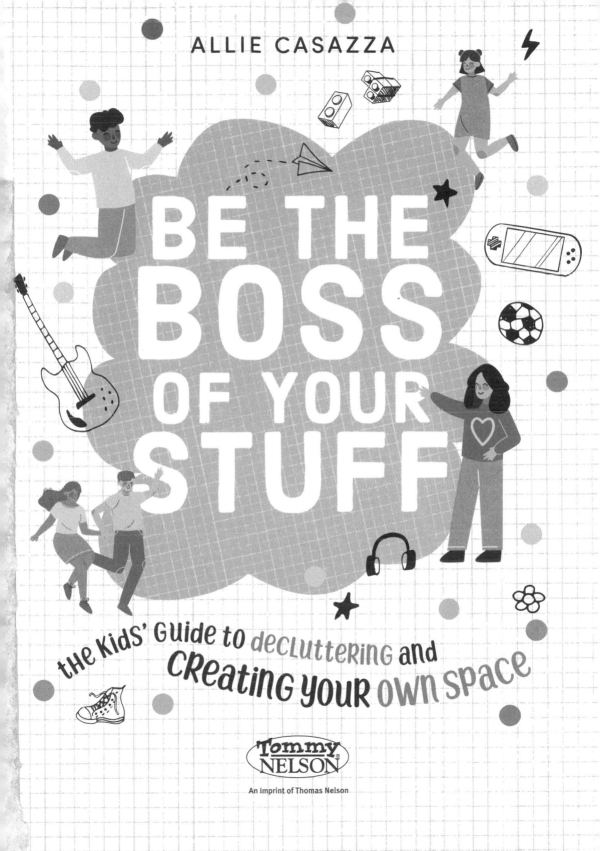

BE THE BOSS OF YOUR STUFF

the Kids' Guide to Decluttering and CReatinG YouR own space

Tommy
NELSON®

An Imprint of Thomas Nelson

To Bella, Leland, Hudson, and Emmett.

You guys are the reason I figured this out, the reason I kept going, the reason I continue to spread the message of simplicity to an overcomplicated, heavy world.

I love you all so much. Keep using your light to make the world a better place.

—Mom

Be the Boss of Your Stuff
© 2022 Allie Casazza
Tommy Nelson, PO Box 141000, Nashville, TN 37214

Published in Nashville, Tennessee, by Tommy Nelson. Tommy Nelson is an imprint of Thomas Nelson. Thomas Nelson is a registered trademark of HarperCollins Christian Publishing, Inc.

Published in association with literary agent Jenni Burke of Illuminate Literary Agency, www.illluminateliterary.com.

Tommy Nelson titles may be purchased in bulk for educational, business, fund-raising, or sales promotional use. For information, please email SpecialMarkets@ThomasNelson.com.

NOTES

Step 3. Get the Trash Out and Check Your Habits

1. *Word Explorer Children's Dictionary*, s.v. "habit," accessed July 25, 2021, https://kids.wordsmyth.net/we /?level=2&rid=18357.

2. Lena Firestone, "Thinking Positively: Why You Need to Wire Your Brain to Think Positive," PsychAlive, acessed July 26, 2021, https://www.psychalive.org/thinking-positively/.

Step 7. Design Your Space

1. "Color Psychology," True Value Paint, accessed July 25, 2021, https://www.truevaluepaint.com/color-101 /color-psychology.

ISBN 978-1-4002-2582-8 (audiobook)
ISBN 978-1-4002-2586-6 (eBook)
ISBN 978-1-4002-2641-2 (HC)

Library of Congress Cataloging-in-Publication Data is on file.

Written by Allie Casazza

Photos © Brian Casazza Photography LLC: pages iv, 4, 19, 25, 41, 72, 79, 80, 100, 109 (blue minimalist bed), 116, 119, 120, 132, 140, 148.

Photos © iStock: pages xii, 2, 30, 52, 54, 108 (colorful pillows on metal bed; green Scandinavian futon), 109 (bedroom with triangles; bedroom with blue curtains; bedroom with cactus pillow), 126, 144 by KatarzynaBialasiewicz; page 9 by wundervisuals; page 34 by BONNINSTUDIO; page 36 by Andrea Colarieti; page 39 by Pongmanat018; page 66 by Aslan Alphan; page 68 by undefined undefined; page 93 by a_namenko; page 95 by skodonnell; page 97 by mixetto; page 108 (macrame decoration) by Olga Romanova; page 108 (antique books) by gemenacom; page 108 (old-fashioned lamp) by baytunc; page 109 (orange lamp) by malerapaso; page 109 (cactus) by nixki; page 146 by PeopleImages.

Photos © Shutterstock: pages 91, 104 (bed), 110, 122 by Photographee.eu; page 104 (unicorn poster) by ebe_dsgn; page 104 (mountains poster) by Mystery Kit; page 104 (brave poster) by S-Victoria; page 108 (country-style bedroom) by jafara; page 108 (fox; bear) by anitapol; page 131 by New Africa.

Printed in the United States of America

22 23 24 25 26 PC/LSCC 6 5 4 3 2

Mfr: LSC / Crawfordsville, IN / June 2022 / PO #12138617

contents

a note for the GROWN-UP

Hi, friend!

I'm honored that you're giving this book to a kid in your life. I have big hopes for this message and its effect on the next generation! Thank you, from the bottom of my heart, for being a tide-turner with me.

Several years ago I had three kids under the age of three. I was a stay-at-home mom, and at that time, I felt so depressed, so overwhelmed, so *stuck* in my home and in my life. Those feelings leaked into everything—how I felt about myself, my parenting, my home, and my relationships. And those negative feelings about my life impacted every aspect of it. I had no idea how to make it better.

Out of desperation I decided to make the physical space around me lighter. I hoped that if the heaviness of my space was transferring to other parts of my life, then maybe the lightness would too. *And I was right.*

I had never realized how much *stuff* my family had

accumulated over the years. We owned so many things we weren't using that just sat on shelves or were stuffed in closets and drawers. And the worst part was that it was all just sitting around for the kids to pull out and make a mess. And so they did. Every day. And then I would pick it all up again and put it away. Over and over and over.

What a cycle! Such an unnecessary time-suck and drain on my mental energy. Our home had an atmosphere of tension because of the disarray, so the kids were constantly bickering, they were overstimulated, and their attitudes were negative. Our system needed to change big-time, and I was ready to make that happen.

As I sifted through each room and got rid of clutter, there was less and less housework to do. I learned a lesson that changed my life moving forward: **what takes up your space takes up your time.**

This journey I went through as a mom has brought so much freedom to my family. The house is easy to maintain, I'm happier, I'm more available for what I actually want to spend my time and energy on, the kids have more time to play, and their toy bins hold only their favorite things—the things worth taking up space. They spend less time on chores and cleanup and more time riding their bikes and skateboarding to the park. Our home feels lighter, and I do too. And since I'm the mom, that lightness spills over to my kids and the vibe in our home.

The simple act of decluttering has changed everything. It taught us that we can have a home that works *with* us, not against us. It also taught us a lot of lessons about consumption—what we buy, why we buy things, and how many things we buy. It's been transformative! I've passed these lessons and this lifestyle of realistic minimalism to my kids, and it's been a really cool thing to see them grow into.

They are less materialistic than many of their friends. They are more grounded—they're happier, they're more confident, and they have more self-control. They are more connected to each other as siblings. Their imaginations have bloomed. (I wish I would have known sooner that kids' brains don't function well when overstimulated by clutter!) They also know who they are as human beings. They've tapped into their talents, interests, and gifts, and they have time to develop them. At such young ages, that is a huge benefit! My kids are now grown up in this lifestyle of simplicity, and it's been nothing but good.

We still do birthday parties. We still celebrate holidays and get excited about presents. It's just less chaotic, less about consumerism, less noisy. It's more aligned with the kind of childhood I deeply desire my kids to experience, and that feels so good.

If you picked up this book, I assume you want your kids to know this freedom too. You probably want them to grow up with an inspired childhood that helps them develop what makes them unique and what makes their imaginations run wild.

As a parent, I have made a lot of mistakes. Haven't we all? But one of the best things I've done for my kids is to let their space be *their* space. Granting them ownership of their stuff and their rooms has given them freedom to be creative and discover who they are.

It's a tricky business to not control the way my kids keep their rooms. It hasn't come naturally to me. But by letting go of that control, their bedrooms have become a safe space that feels like theirs. It's a small way I can send the message that they're different from me and that they are their own selves—and that's *good*!

Yes, there are boundaries. There are rules in the home. They can't keep an old plate of tuna under their bed or re-wear the same pair of underwear twelve times and not hear about it from me. Like, don't be gross. But they *can* have art all over their walls if that's what they want. It doesn't have to be magazine-ready. It doesn't even have to reflect our standards for the rest of the house. Our job as grown-ups is to teach them, using pieces of freedom as part of the process.

By empowering our kids to **be the boss of their stuff,** we give them a taste of freedom that's so encouraging for kids. They crave independence but can't totally have it yet. They want to feel like they're contributing to the family. It's time to teach them responsibility by giving little bits of freedom. Having their own space is a huge way to allow them to feel those things, even if they share a room with a sibling.

I've been teaching minimalism for over ten years. I've helped hundreds of thousands of moms transform their homes and lives. If you feel like *you* need to simplify, streamline, and take action in this way too, please know I am here to support you! It's what I do every day in my books, in my online programs, and in my podcast, *The Purpose Show*.

Your Uncluttered Home®, my online course that helps clear clutter and reduce stress, will transform your space and your life. My first book, *Declutter Like a Mother*, will walk you through so many positive changes in your mind-set and your home. And if you'd like support in communicating this lifestyle to your child, check out the program I created with child-play therapist Amy Tirpak called Uncluttered Kids®. It's everything you need to completely shift your family's lifestyle to something much simpler and more sustainable, with less chaos, stress, and clutter, and more joy and energy to focus on what really matters.

I wrote this book for every kid—kids of all personalities, gifts, weaknesses, strengths, genders, and backgrounds. It's meant to help them realize the beauty and potential hidden in their spaces. My intention is to help you empower your kids to have a more minimalistic mind set that they'll carry into adulthood. What a beautiful gift that is for them—and for you too.

The benefits kids get from this minimalist lifestyle is nearly limitless. It discourages a sense of entitlement. It encourages creativity, playfulness, and wild imaginations. It helps them develop social skills and healthy habits. It breeds happiness, gratitude, and an awareness of charitable giving. It increases the desire to spend time outdoors, and it brings so much more peace into the home.

I'm going to walk your kids through a process that has helped hundreds of thousands of women radically simplify and change their lives. Your kids will

- come up with a plan for how they want their room to look and feel,
- remove clutter and understand the negative effects of it,
- develop a solid plan for storing what they're keeping and the lifelong habit of being tidy,
- learn what to do with all their artwork and papers,
- confidently design their spaces,
- create a plan for keeping their spaces clean,
- get a basic understanding of mindful consumption of goods,
- learn how to use their extra space and time to grow their dreams,
- understand how their physical spaces affect their moods and actions, and
- learn how to honor themselves through the way they care for their stuff.

Raising my kids with less—less clutter, less stress, less chaos, less unnecessary junk—has been one of the greatest gifts I've ever given them and inadvertently given myself.

I'm on your side. I'm rooting for you. And I'm so proud of you for picking up this book. You're doing a great job. You are a gift to your kid.

Rooting for you always,
XO ALLIE

> ## Resources
>
> Check out these resources to further support you and your family: Your Uncluttered Home® and Uncluttered Kids®. You can also go to alliecasazza .com/grownups for more information and a readers-only deal on both of these amazing programs. And check out my first book, written for moms, *Declutter Like a Mother.* For more information, go to https:// declutterlikeamother.com.

WHat you need to Know

Hi, kiddo!

We're about to go on a really cool journey together. It's going to help you so much! My name is Allie, and it's my job to help people **be the boss of their stuff** so their stuff doesn't become the boss of them. That may seem kind of strange, but it's true!

A few years ago, my kids had *tons* of toys and lots of other stuff too. The toys were everywhere, but my kids didn't really play with them all. They had so many clothes that we couldn't close their dresser drawers. Their rooms were always messy, and they would be overwhelmed when it was time to clean up. It was hard for them to focus on things like reading and homework because the space around them was so messy.

Sometimes my kids would whine and complain because it

would take so long to clean up and do chores. So we decided to fix the problem. We grabbed some boxes and got rid of all the stuff we didn't really love or need, including any toys that my kids didn't love. After that, they were *excited* to be in their rooms because they felt so much happier in there! It took *way* less time to clean up and do chores, they were able to easily find their favorite toys to play with, and they even noticed their attitudes were better.

Then I started helping other families make their homes happier. I got so good at it that it became my job! I started making videos and podcast episodes to help other people change their homes and change their lives. So now I'm a pro!

When we surround ourselves with too much stuff, not only does it make our rooms and spaces messy, but it can make us feel messy too. It's like we're being bossed around by our stuff instead of being in charge of it. I want you to know that I'm here to help you take control of that stuff and become the boss of it. You'll like your room better and feel lighter in life—everything will feel less messy. And if you follow what's in this book, things are about to get so much simpler.

CLUTTER IS THE PROBLEM

Imagine this. It's a beautiful sunny day, and all your friends are playing outside. You want to join in on the fun, but you've got some things to get done first. Like homework and chores. The clock is ticking till dinner. What if...

- You sit down in a space that's clean and neat. Everything is where you need it to be. You have plenty of room for your books, papers, pencils, and computer. You knock out your work with a clear space and a clear mind. Then...
- You finish your chores in five minutes or less. You made your bed this morning, and you picked up your room after you played yesterday. You take your laundry to the laundry room, do a little bit of tidying, and even help your mom with some family spaces. Then...
- Boom! It's time to have fun.

Now, doesn't that sound better than this?

- You sit down to do homework, and your space is covered in clutter—papers, toys, books, and other random things. You can't find a pencil. You lose ten minutes before you even get started. Then . . .

- You look around your room and feel overwhelmed, maybe even tired, just from being in there—but especially when it's time to clean up. You think, *This is going to take forever!* And you want to give up before you even start. Then . . .

- You realize you'd need a shovel to clear a path to the bed. You don't know where to start, and by the time you're even close to being done, all your friends have gone home for the afternoon.

If the first scenario sounds like your typical day, you're going to love this book. And if the second scenario sounds like you, you're going to love it even more! I'm going to show you how to get rid of clutter so you can focus on what you love. We all need help getting a handle on clutter and stuff, whether we're already the boss of it or it's totally the boss of us.

WHO'S tHE BOSS?

What kind of emotions do you typically feel when you're simply spending time in your room?

a. Happy and peaceful.

b. Stressed and frustrated.

c. Like you don't want to be in there.

What kind of emotions do you typically feel when it's time to clean up your room?

a. I'm confident. I know it's going to be easy.

b. I'm annoyed.

c. I'm overwhelmed. I know it's going to take *forever*.

How much time does it take you to clean your room completely, from start to finish?

a. Less than 10 minutes.

b. About 20–30 minutes.

c. More than 30 minutes.

How much of the stuff in your room is your favorite?

a. Everything. I don't have much, but the things I do have are my absolute favorites.

b. I know what my favorites are, but I also have a lot more.

c. I have favorites, but they are surrounded by all kinds of other things.

How easy is it for you to find something you're looking for in your room?

a. Super easy!
b. It takes me a minute or two.
c. It takes forever, and I might not ever find it.

How often do things go missing in your room?

a. Never.
b. Sometimes.
c. All the time.

How easy is it for you to focus on schoolwork or reading in your room?

a. It's very easy to focus!
b. It's somewhat easy. I struggle sometimes.
c. It's impossible to focus in there. I do schoolwork in another room.

How hard will it be for you to get rid of some of your things?

a. No problem. I'm ready!
b. I'm a little nervous but ready to make things better.
c. This will be difficult for me. I get overwhelmed when I think about getting rid of some of my things.

if you got MOSTLY a's

Then you're already becoming a boss! Continue reading to learn even more tips and secrets on how to become a great boss of your stuff.

if you got MOSTLY B's

Then you're getting there, but it's a bit of a struggle. You're *so* ready to figure out how to get clutter under control so you can be a boss of your stuff.

if you got MOSTLY C's

Then you won't want to put down this book! You're going to learn a lot about decluttering and creating your own space. But don't worry—even most adults haven't figured all of this out yet. That means you're ahead of the game because you're starting the process of becoming a boss of your stuff and your space.

What if you had more time to do the things you love to do? Like skateboarding, playing video games, riding your bike or scooter, or playing with your friends. If there were less cleaning to do, if you were able to focus better when doing homework because there's less mess around you, then you'd have more time for fun!

Because my son Leo doesn't have to spend more than five to ten minutes cleaning his room each day, he can make the choice to go skateboarding with his friend who lives down the street. Because my daughter, Bella, can quickly pick up her room (instead of it taking over an hour and causing lots of tears like it used to!), she can make the choice to play on the trampoline before dinner or work on her sketching.

If you've ever felt stressed out when you've walked
    into your room . . .
If you've ever spent a stupid amount of time looking
    for things you need or want . . .
If you've ever felt like you couldn't focus on your
    homework . . .
If cleaning your room takes *so long* and you don't
    understand why your grown-up wants you to
    clean it before you play . . .

You're not alone! The problem is clutter. And it's being the boss of you.

BE THE BOSS OF CLUTTER

Clutter is the stuff in your room that you don't use very much, don't need to have, or don't love. Clutter is like the bad dude in a movie—it's always making your life harder and getting in your way. It takes up space, makes your cleanup time longer, and makes your room feel messy—even after you've cleaned!

Our family cut our cleaning time by *more than half* just by getting rid of clutter! When you have a bunch of stuff, you have more to put away and more to move around when you're looking for something. More stuff equals more time spent cleaning.

Imagine spending only a few minutes cleaning your room and having all that extra time to do something fun.

How much time do you spend picking up your room
every week?

How much time do you think you spend looking for lost
items?

Are you okay with how much time you spend
cleaning your room and looking for stuff?

Having too much stuff can affect how you feel too. It can make your brain freak out, leaving you super stressed and in a bad mood. For example, have you noticed that it's almost impossible to study when you have a bunch of stuff all over your room? Even if it's hidden in a closet, you know it's there. You can't concentrate when your brain keeps nagging you about the things that need to be put away. Clutter makes it hard to get your homework done, and you spend more time on it than you would if the clutter were gone. All that stuff in your room even makes it hard for you to focus on playing and having fun or hanging out with your friends.

So if clutter is such a problem, how do we end up with all

HOW DO WE end UP WitH aLL tHiS Stuff?

Think back for a minute to your last birthday or Christmas. How many presents did you get? Now, out of those, how many do you use or play with every day? Every week?

Is it possible that you received more gifts than you actually have the time and space to use? We're going to keep talking about stuff—how we get it, what we should get, and how to **be the boss** of it. For now, write down three of your favorite gifts you've received in the last year. (And *favorite means you use it and enjoy it a lot.*)

1. _____

2. _____

3. _____

this stuff? Well, it's actually pretty easy to end up with too much stuff. Think about it. One minute you see an ad for a cool toy, and the next minute you're trying to figure out how to save your money to get it. But when you actually *do* get the toy, it only makes you happy for a couple of days; then you stop playing with it as much, maybe never again, and it becomes clutter.

When we have a room that's totally **stuffed** with **stuff**, the stuff isn't fun anymore. We have too much, and now we have to be responsible for cleaning it up all the time. I don't want to spend my Saturdays organizing my toys and cleaning out my drawers. I'd rather just not buy things I don't really love and play with my favorite things I already own. The small moments of feeling excited for something new aren't worth what it takes to keep my room clean.

Look around your room. Notice where all your toys, clothes, and school supplies are. Look under your bed and inside your closet. How much of your brain do you think is clogged up by the way your room looks right now?

What if the reason some of your homework has been hard is because you can't focus while your room is messy? It's not cool for clutter to be taking up space in your brain when you need your brain to do math and be creative. How much of your brain do you **want** to be taken up by your cluttered room?

A long time ago I didn't know any of this. My room was a giant mess. I had piles of clothes on the floor and on the bed. I had stacks of books leaning against the walls. Dust bunnies lived under my bed and in the corners of the room. Shoes were everywhere, and I always tripped over them. It was a mess. I left it that way for a long time because I didn't want to clean it up. And I didn't know it was bothering my brain and putting me in a bad mood.

One day I got sick of it and cleaned it all up. I put all the trash in the trash can. I gave away all the stuff I didn't like anymore. I put all the books on a shelf, I put my shoes on a closet shelf, I dusted the dust bunnies, and I put away all my things where they belonged.

The next day I felt so excited that I didn't want to leave my room. I even wanted to have breakfast in my room because it was so clean! It made me feel so good. Why? Well, just as clutter makes your brain feel heavy and stressed, having no clutter makes it feel *awesome*.

Here's what you need to know: you are the boss of your space and your stuff. What does being the boss mean? Being the boss *does not* mean wearing important clothes and sitting at a big desk. It means that you're the one in charge. And if you're in charge, you want to do a good job with what you are in charge of. Being the boss means making decisions about what things stay and what things leave; it's deciding what's important and what's not.

Because you're growing up and you're an older kid now, you get to decide how your room feels and what it looks like, and you are also responsible for keeping it clean.

I'm going to be your new best friend because I'm going to teach you how to be a great boss and I'm going to help you make your room look awesome—your brain won't have to focus on the mess anymore. Not only will your room be clean and clutter-free, but it will be uniquely *yours*, and the stuff you keep in it will be stuff that makes you happy. You're never going to want to leave.

This book was written for you and your room. I created it so that you won't have to spend so much time cleaning and so you

Draw a picture of yourself as the boss of your room, the boss of your stuff. You can be wearing whatever you want to wear, you can be in your room or not—whatever you think it looks like to be the boss of your space.

have more time to focus on being you—an awesome kid with a lot of gifts and dreams.

And you know what? My kids are going to help you too!

Bella and Leland are about your age. They spend less than two minutes cleaning their rooms every day because they don't want clutter being sneaky and taking all their time. They spend all their extra time playing outside, playing video games, and drawing, and they're able to finish their schoolwork super fast because their brains are happier without clutter.

They're going to help me teach you how to make your room like this too. You'll see notes and tips from them throughout the book.

The next thing we need to do is come up with a plan for your room. 'Cause without a plan, this will be a lot harder.

Let's go!

PLAN
YOUR ROOM

We know that clutter is a problem. It causes you to spend more time cleaning and less time having fun. Having too much stuff affects how you feel, distracts you from doing what you want to do, and puts you in a bad mood.

You're going to get back to being in charge because this is your space. If you want to play more and clean less, you should be able to do that—the secret is to get rid of the clutter. Most adults don't know how to do the stuff that you're learning in this book right now, so becoming the boss of your stuff now is going to put you way ahead of the game.

A couple of years ago, Bella was starting to get really good at drawing. All she wanted to do was draw. She was filling sketch pads every single day, and she loved it. But every time I would tell her she needed to clean her room, she would get so frustrated because she was right in the middle of drawing and didn't want to stop to clean her room.

I realized she was getting so frustrated about cleaning her room because of how long it took. I asked her, "If it took you only five minutes to clean your room, would you still be upset that you had to do it?" Her answer? She wanted it to take even less time! But there was only one way she could spend less time cleaning—she'd have to have less stuff. Because, as we know, **what takes up your space takes up your time.** So Bella and I came up with a plan for her room. We talked about how she wanted her space to look and feel so she could do the things she loved. And if her room wasn't helping her do what she loved, then it wasn't fulfilling its purpose.

Think of all those times you've been frustrated that you had to clean your room. Remember how overwhelming it felt? Remember all the emotions it brought up? Can you see yourself standing in the middle of your room, not knowing where to start because stuff was everywhere? Are toys and books piled on top of the dresser and spilling off the side? Are you frustrated because you have things all over the floor and spilling out of your closet—and you don't even know where to put them?

What if it were *impossible* for your room to get that crazy again? It can be! But you have to get rid of the junk.

Before we get the clutter out, we have to do one super important thing first. **We have to make a plan for your room!**

Draw a picture of your room. Include everything that's sitting out that should be put away, anything disorganized, and the stuff that bothers you. Under the drawing, make a list of what you think needs to change about your room.

MAKING A PLAN FOR YOU AND YOUR ROOM

This is where you get to be the boss of your space. You're going to decide how you want your room to look and feel, what you want to use your room for, and what kinds of things you want in this space.

Bosses get to make decisions, and that's what you're doing today.

If you share a room with someone else in your house, no worries! You're still in charge of your stuff. You're still in charge of how long it takes you to clean up your part. And you can still create a space that allows you to have time for what's important to you.

Now, to get more specific and make smart decisions when it comes to your room, ask yourself some questions. Have you ever seen a cool bedroom on TV or the internet that you really liked? What made it seem cool to you? I'm guessing it wasn't a pile of dirty clothes in the middle of the floor. What about the toys and decorations in the room? They probably weren't tossed about the room either. Everything in the room was chosen and placed on purpose. Picture the most awesome bedroom you can think of and then follow these steps:

1. First, walk into your room right now without doing anything to it. How do you feel when you walk in?

_____

_____

_____

2. Then, imagine walking into your new room, the one you're going to create as you read this book. This room looks awesome and has all your favorite things. How do you *want* to feel when you walk into your new room?

Here are some words to help get you started:

Adventurous	Excited for the day	Proud
Brave	Fun	Quiet
Calm	Happy	Ready for anything
Creative	**Playful**	Strong

Write down how you want to feel as soon as you walk through the doorway!

_____

_____

_____

3. Now think about what you actually *need* to have in your room.

    You have to have some things in your space to be able to live in it, like your bed and your dresser. Make a list of things you need in your room to help you remember what your room is for and how you will use it.

    Remember, you don't need to list *everything* in your room right now. After all, you haven't gotten the clutter out yet! List only the things you *need* in your room so we can start from a clean slate.

_____

_____

_____

4. What do you *want* your room to have in it?

    The answer to this question is different for every person because we each have unique personalities and interests.

    For example, Bella is super creative and *loves* spending alone time in her room. She prefers to keep all her toys in her room, doesn't mind messes, and spends most of her time creating art at her disorganized desk. Bella uses her room for everything except eating. She plays in there, sleeps in there, and creates in there.

Leland, on the other hand, likes things clean. He's more organized and structured. He has the brain of a builder or an engineer, so he's always thinking. He prefers to have his toys kept out of sight in a bin with a lid and to store his LEGOs in another room completely so his room isn't too full. He spends hours building and drawing plans for cities in his sketchbook. He uses his room for rest, sleep, and getting ready for his day—and that's about it.

What about you? What kind of person are you when you're in your room? Your space should be set up to help you be that person. We want to get rid of things that make it harder for you to enjoy your space, and we want to set up your room to make it unique to who *you* are. It's your room, after all.

Write out what you want your room to have in it.

Examples: I want my room to have space for me to draw as much as I want. I want a big toy bin so I can keep my things in my own space. I want to have the coziest blanket and a bookshelf because I love to snuggle and read.

_____

_____

_____

_____

KNOWING WHO YOU ARE

The most important thing in planning for your room is knowing who you are. When you know what you like and dislike and what you want to do with your free time, you can make smart choices for your room.

Bella likes being in her room because the style is hers and she feels comfortable in there. She feels inspired.

Having an art desk makes her want to be in her room and makes her want to create art a lot. However, she has a hard time doing schoolwork in her room because her paint, colored pencils, and drawings distract her. So she does schoolwork downstairs at the kitchen table where she can focus.

a note from Bella

Your room should be set up for *you*!

I love art. That's my thing. My desk is set up with art supplies and sketch pads so I can get creative when I'm not doing schoolwork.

So what about you?

If you like to play with Hot Wheels, you could have space on the floor for your cars and the tracks you build.

If you're into building with LEGOs, your room could have a table to build on and a shelf to display your creations, plus bins to organize the LEGO pieces.

If you like to sing and listen to music, you could have a karaoke microphone and a speaker or headphones so you can listen to tunes while you play.

If you're a writer, you could have a desk with paper ready to use for when you get inspired.

Make sure you feel comfortable in your room and design your room in a way that will make you love it!

Bella knows who she is. She is confident in that. She sets her room up to reflect *her*.

Because Bella is an artist, she likes to have art by other professional artists on her walls to keep her inspired and focused on her goal of becoming a professional artist. She also doesn't have tons of toys like she used to because it crowded her room and brain and made it difficult for her to have time to work on her art and focus on anything.

She has a bin at the foot of her bed that holds only the toys she really looks forward to playing with and plays with often. Those are the toys that she feels are worth keeping and worth taking up space and time to clean.

Let's think through this together.

What are your strengths? What are you really good at?

_____

_____

What do you love to spend time doing?

_____

_____

What do you struggle with? What are the hardest parts of your day?

Example: *If you struggle with focusing on your homework, look at the space where you normally sit when you do your homework and see if it's full of distractions, like too many books, toys, trash, or art supplies. If this space just doesn't work for doing homework, think of another place you could do it and ask your grown-up if you can change your space or if they'll help you to create a better homework station. Maybe the kitchen table would work better for you, or maybe a guest room. or even the trampoline in the sunshine could be a better fit.*

_____

_____

tHiS, Not tHat

Check out these lists to see what makes a good homework spot—and what doesn't!

THIS
- At a clean table or desk
- In a room without distractions
- Outside in the sunlight
- With a snack and a glass of water

NOT THAT
- At the kitchen table next to this morning's dishes and mysterious crusty stuff
- In the same room your sister is playing video games
- In a dark room that makes you feel sad and bored
- When you're tired and hungry

If you struggle with falling asleep at night, try getting your room to feel more peaceful before you go to sleep. Pick up your clothes and turn the lights down. My kids have a projector light that turns their bedroom into a night sky with blue swirls that dance on the ceiling. It creates the peaceful vibe at night that helps them relax and drift off to sleep.

So what problems does your room have? What can you do to make your room feel calmer?

_____

_____

How can you make these changes in your room? Let's brainstorm some ideas!

_____

_____

_____

Now share your ideas with your grown-up.

CHORE CHECKLIST

If you struggle to remember to do your chores, put a chart on the wall in your room where you'll easily see it. This is an awesome way to have a visual checklist of items that help you keep your room in order. It can help you do your homework more effectively and efficiently. It can help you play better. And it can even help you fall asleep faster.

Try creating your own chore checklist.

☐ Make the bed.

☐ Put away clean clothes.

☐ Throw the dirty clothes in a hamper or laundry room.

☐ Put away books and toys.

☐ Throw away trash.

☐ _____

☐ _____

☐ _____

☐ _____

USING YOUR IMAGINATION TO
MAKE YOUR ROOM EPIC

Now that you have a clearer picture of how you want your room to work, let's dive deeper into your imagination and use it to create your dream room.

List all your favorite things.

Examples: *Cats, dragons, art, baseball,* Star Wars, *black-and-white photos, or science.*

_____

_____

Use your list of favorite things and pick something (or several things) that you would love to have in your room. For example, if your favorite thing is cats, you could have your grown-up help you find a cool cat pillow to go on your bed. You might also add a cat calendar or a cat notepad for your desk. Or if science is one of your favorite things, you might find a chart of the periodic table to put on the wall or buy a robotics kit and place it on your desk.

What favorite things do you want to include when designing your room?

_____

_____

By answering these questions, you can figure out what makes you, _you_. Then you can use your lists of favorite things to make a good plan for your room.

Use the space below to brainstorm other things you love and would want to bring into your room. Use your wild imagination!

_____

_____

Draw a picture of how you want your room to look. You'll use this picture as we go through the other chapters in this book and continue the process of making your room look awesome. If you hold on to the feeling of how you want your room to look and feel, it will help you make decisions about what to keep and what to get rid of.

As you draw, be sure to look through all the lists from this chapter so you can remember all the big ideas we talked about.

- Think about what you need in your room, what you want in your room, and how you want your room to feel when you walk in.
- Consider what you're good at and what you're interested in.
- Think about the problems your room has right now and what parts need to change.
- And remember not to crowd your room—because the more stuff you have, the more time you have to spend taking care of it!

Get the trash out and check your habits

the first step to transforming any space is, as an artist might say, to start with as blank of a canvas as possible. And the easiest things to start removing are the things that can be thrown away. In other words, grab a trash bag!

It's so easy for trash to collect in your room. Crumpled papers, wrappers from Halloween candy, broken pencils behind your bed, packaging from new toys—it all adds up, and it's time to get it out.

GET IT OUT!

Trash is the easiest clutter to get rid of, so it's a great place to start making more space. (And getting rid of trash makes you feel good, which will motivate you to keep going!)

Here are the types of trash we're looking for today:

- Old, broken toys
- Pieces of things that you have no idea what they belong to (Check with a grown-up to be sure it's actually trash!)
- Old food and wrappers
- Empty, used sandwich and snack bags
- Juice boxes, water bottles, and soda cans
- Pieces of paper stuffed under furniture (We'll handle actual paperwork later!)
- Random stuff you can't use anymore, like old, worn-out shoelaces or dried-out glue

Go get a trash bag (or two!) and start by the door to your room. Do you see any trash just lying on the floor? In the corners of the room? Under your furniture? Start there and put it all in the bag.

REMINDER: There are two types of trash—recyclable and nonrecyclable. Recyclable trash is stuff like plastic bags, plastic water bottles, cardboard containers, old clothing, and clear plastic lids. Be sure to recycle what you can when cleaning up your space!

Next, open all the drawers in your room and check for trash there, bagging it up as you go.

You might find trash hidden in the back corners of your desk drawers or stuffed in the top drawer of your dresser next to your socks. **Wherever it is, get it out!** Remember, trash is a part of clutter, and clutter is a time-stealing, brain-killing bad dude! It has to go.

When Bella and I were first decluttering her room, we found a bunch of trash in her socks-and-underwear drawer! It was so random and funny. Who puts trash in their underwear drawer? But apparently it can happen, so be sure to check just in case.

CREATE GOOD HABITS

Do you know what habits are? An online dictionary for kids describes it this way:

Habit (ha-bət):

1. A regular action; routine.
   His habit is to brush his teeth before putting on his pajamas.
2. A fixed, repeated action, often done without meaning to or wanting to.
   She has an annoying habit of tapping her toes.[1]

What habits have you formed while living in your room? While you're getting the trash out, pay attention to where you've left all that trash.

Do you eat in your room, then leave trash behind? Do you draw at your desk, then leave the colored pencils out, causing them to roll off and get stuck behind the desk? Do you always put your shoes by your door when you walk in from school?

Once you've noticed your habits, check to see what type of habits they are. There are helpful habits and hurtful habits.

Helpful habits make life easier and happier.

Hurtful habits make life harder and more frustrating.

A helpful habit could be something like getting your homework done before dinnertime. Picture this:

- Every day you come home from school and get a healthy snack and a big glass of water.
- You go to your clean workstation, and you knock out your homework.
- You put everything back in your backpack, and you put your backpack where it goes (on a hook by the door, on the desk in your room, at the bottom of your closet—you get the idea). Your work is neatly packed in the bag, and the bag is in the same place every time.

This helpful habit helps so many things! Not only do you get to go out and play, but you can do so without dreading more work to do when you get in. Plus, you don't have to worry about losing your work or rushing around in the morning looking for your stuff. This healthy habit takes away stress!

A hurtful habit could be something like leaving a mess in your room. Imagine this:

- Every time you eat in your room, you forget to throw away the trash or take your dishes back to the kitchen.
- Then you do it again and again. And because you make a mess every time, the mess keeps growing.
- Before you know it, there's a pile of sticky, crumbly grossness you have to clean up.

Why are we talking about habits while you're working on removing the trash from your room? Because getting rid of habits that aren't helping you is a lot like getting rid of the trash that's not helping you love your room. We are cleaning things up, inside and outside!

What are some helpful habits that you have right now?

Example: *Every time I finish my homework, I immediately put it in my backpack for school the next day.*

_____

_____

What are some hurtful habits you have right now that make life frustrating and more difficult? (Secret shortcut: Look around your room for trash and clutter piles for hints at what some hurtful habits might be!)

Examples: *When I get home from school, I drop my backpack on the floor, and my papers spill out. I leave my towel on the floor after I shower, even after my grown-up said not to.*

_____

_____

How would you feel if you changed all of your hurtful habits? How would your life change?

_____

_____

Make Simple Changes

Here's some good news: you can turn hurtful habits into helpful habits! I do this all the time, and it's really easy.

I used to have a hurtful habit that made my house look cluttered. All that clutter made me feel tired even when it was the middle of the day. Whenever I was downstairs and had some-thing that needed to be put away upstairs, I would just set it on the floor by the stairs to be taken up later. But I never would take it upstairs, so it just sat there all day.

I decided to turn this hurtful habit into a helpful one by putting a basket at the bottom of the stairs. Every time I had something that needed to be put away upstairs, I put it in the basket instead of on the floor. It didn't look cluttered anymore, and I could carry the basket upstairs each night and put my things away where they belonged.

I turned a hurtful habit into a helpful habit just by making a simple change—adding a basket.

What would work for you? Maybe you can put a trash can in your room or eat somewhere else in your house.

What are some ways you can turn your hurtful habits into helpful habits?

_____

_____

_____

a note from Bella

After my mom and I found all the trash I had been stashing in my socks-and-underwear drawer, we decided to put a small trash can next to my dresser. That way, anytime I was using the top of my dresser to write in my journal or draw in my sketch pad and needed somewhere to put my trash, the trash can was right there. Having a trash can nearby kept me from cramming crumpled papers into my drawers or walking to another room to find a trash can (which I never really did!). It's really helpful to find ways to support your habit rather than have to learn a new one.

How can you change things in your room (like I did by adding a basket) to help you create helpful habits instead of hurtful ones? You're in charge of how you act, so what do you want to change about the way you use your room? (Remember, the trash in your space can show you a lot about your habits!)

_____

_____

_____

_____

_____

When you're done getting all the trash out of your room and into the garbage bags and recycle bin, take a moment to think through the process.

What kinds of trash did you find in your room? When you write it all down, you can better understand how much junk was taking up your space.

_____

_____

_____

At this point, do you see a connection between your room's atmosphere (or feeling) and how you have been feeling when you're in your room? For example, if your room has been messy and crowded, then you might have been feeling overwhelmed and antsy.

_____

_____

_____

Now take the bags out to the trash bins or have a grown-up help you do that. Sometimes when you're finishing something, it's easy to get a little lazy. Fighting clutter is hard work! Push through to the end and make sure you get *all* the trash *all* the way out of your room and into the main trash bin.

It feels so good to have all that junk out of your space!

Now that the trash is out of your room, we want to create a solution to the problem that caused all that trash to pile up in the first place. Just like Bella and I came up with a solution for her trash problem by putting a trash can in her room, you can find a solution for you too. Here are a few questions to consider:

- Is there already a trash can in there?
- Do you need to move the trash can to a better place?
- Do you need a bigger trash can or one with a lid?
- Do you need a trash can liner to keep the can clean?

Talk to your grown-up about anything you need help with.

How can you make getting rid of the trash in your room a little easier? What ideas can you come up with?

_____

_____

_____

_____

CReate a new HaBit

Have you ever tried to form a new habit? It can be really hard! And we often get stuck by thinking, *If I just have enough motivation, I'll start my new habit.* But there's a trick to getting a new habit to stick—you need a plan!

New habit you want to create:
Examples: *You want to start reading more, practicing playing guitar every day, begin journaling, or remembering to put your dirty clothes in the hamper.*

_____

Time of day that works best for this new habit:
Examples: *Right before school, when you walk into your classroom, before dinner, or before bed.*

_____

Get really specific about what you need for this habit and where you'll do this habit:
Example: *If you want to practice playing your guitar, then you'll need your guitar, a lessons book, a pick, and thirty minutes set aside for practice.*

_____

Now tie this new habit with something you already do. This will make the habit easier for your brain to remember.

Example: *If you want to read a chapter of your book every morning, start reading after something you already do in the morning, like eating breakfast.*

_____

Now put it all together!

EXAMPLE

Who: I

What: will write in my journal

Where: at my desk

When: every morning after I brush my teeth

Why: so that I can think positive thoughts each morning

Now you try it!

Who:

What:

Where:

When:

Why:

Write it in sentence form here:

_____

_____

Now every night before bed, say the sentence above aloud. That will help your brain remember it the next day, and soon you'll have a brand-new habit!

Choose the Positive Over the Negative

How you treat your room affects you, and knowing this gives you a head start in life. Really! You're becoming a decluttering superstar!

I want to explain something else to you that will help you create the room you need and want. It's all about feelings.

People can have positive feelings and negative feelings. Everything that you do in your room and everything that you bring into your room can either make you feel good or bad, positive or negative.

Imagine you are reading your favorite book or playing with your favorite toy alone on your bed with your favorite snack. You're having the *best* day. How do you feel? Probably happy, peaceful, and relaxed, right? Those are examples of positive feelings.

Negative feelings are caused by stuff that puts you in a bad mood.

For example, having a bunch of clutter in your space can give you negative feelings. It can make you tired or grumpy, and it can make you feel like you don't have enough space to play. You might feel overwhelmed when you think of how much time you'll spend cleaning when you'd rather hang out with your friends. Or you could feel stressed because you know your grown-up could come in at any second and tell you to clean up the mess. Those are negative feelings.

We want your room to do two things for you:

1. Help you have more positive feelings.
2. Be a help to you when you have negative feelings (because sometimes those feelings are just a part of life).

Imagine you've had a bad day at school, but you go home, go into your room, and feel so good in there. Your room feels happy, it's clean, and there's no clutter. You can think, play, stretch out on your bed, and relax. That is an example of your room helping you out when you have negative feelings. Your room should be tidy and designed the way you love so that it makes you feel happy. That way, just walking into your room will help put you in a better mood.

Discover the Magic in Your Words

Let's talk about something else that can help you make your room (and your life) even more awesome: words. Good habits can help you keep the trash out of your room, but they can do even more than that. You can have good habits in the ways that you think and talk. Not only do we need to clean the trash out of our rooms, but we need to clean it out of our minds too! Just like we can have the bad habit of letting trash pile up in our physical spaces, we can have the bad habit of letting negative thoughts pile up in our minds.

Anytime you feel like you don't measure up, you're not good enough, you'll never figure something out, you'll never keep your room clean, or you'll never get your grades up, remember that these negative feelings are *all trash*. They're not true! But we all think like this sometimes, and we all need to toss that trash out of our minds just like we toss it out of our rooms.

You can actually create good habits that use the power of your words to change the way you think about yourself, which will then change the way you treat your room. Because the way you treat your room is kind of the way you treat yourself. And I want you to feel great about both.

Good habits + positive words = better feelings (and sometimes cleaner rooms!)

Make a list of positive words. As you write each word, notice how it makes you feel.

Examples: *Bravery, love, joy, play, or strength.*

_____

_____

_____

_____

Now make a list of things that make you happy.

Examples: *Dogs, ballet, friends, soccer, or music.*

_____

_____

_____

_____

We're going to use what we know about words and what we now know about positive and negative feelings to help your brain work in a more positive way. When you repeat positive things out loud, your brain literally changes—and in the best way! Positive words help your brain work better, and each one helps your brain create its own kind of habit. When your brain thinks something positive, it creates a neural pathway that makes it easier for you to think positive thoughts.[2] That just means that positive thoughts lead to more positive thoughts, which make you feel good and improve your day! And who doesn't want that?

Ready to try it?

Repeat these sentences to yourself and see if they make you feel good. If they do, you can repeat these sentences to yourself every morning.

I am an awesome kid.

I can have an awesome, clean room.

I take care of myself and my things.

My room is my safe space, my fun space, and my rest space.

I don't put things in my room that give me negative feelings.

My room makes me feel happy and calm, and this helps me love others.

My room is a place that reminds me how special and loved I am.

Get a piece of paper and write down some of these sentences or your own positive sentences. Focus especially on the ones that make you feel really good. Sometimes the best way to clean up those negative thoughts is to simply replace them with something positive. So copy those good thoughts down on paper and put the paper where you will see it every day. Maybe tape it to your bathroom mirror, put it in a frame above your bed, or put it on your desk where you'll see it before you do homework.

Keep saying those positive words. They will help fuel you to create good habits, and the combination will help you have lighter, happier feelings. Toss the trash and focus on the good!

Get the unused Stuff out

now that we've gotten rid of all the trash in your room, it's time to find another big type of clutter—the *unused* stuff. This type of clutter can be really tricky. You might own a lot of toys that *could* be played with, you have clothes that you *could* wear, or you have a lot of books you *might* read. But the truth is, you *don't* play with those toys or wear those clothes. Those books are just sitting there collecting dust. These things no longer serve a purpose. And that's okay. We *all* have unused clutter, and the solution is simple—get rid of it.

HOW TO GET RID OF UNUSED CLUTTER

Make space on your floor or on your bed to create a pile of stuff you're ready to go through and get rid of. Ask your parent for a bag that you can use to load up things you want to give away.

Keep in mind, we're skipping papers and artwork for now. We'll be tackling that in another chapter.

As you begin, I have a few important and helpful questions you can ask yourself to help you make smart decisions about what to keep in your space.

1. If this object went missing, would I notice and be really sad? Or would I not even notice because it's not important to me?

This question can help you figure out if an item is important to you or not. Sometimes we think something is important to us, but when it goes missing, we don't even notice. And that means we don't need to make space for it in our rooms or our lives.

As you go through your things, pick up each item and ask yourself, *Would I notice if this went missing?* If the words *No, I wouldn't notice* pop into your brain, then put it in a "toss or give-away" pile. If you think, *Yes, I would definitely notice; that would make me very sad,* then put it in a "keep" pile. This is where all the things you choose to keep will go while you are making decisions.

2. How often do I play with this or use it?

Look around your room. What items do you see that you used to love that you don't play with anymore? Maybe you used to always play with that toy drum that your aunt gave you. But now that you think about it, it's just been sitting there for months. Or maybe you used to love taking that stuffed animal everywhere you went, but now you can't even remember the last time you picked it up. It's probably not important enough to keep taking up space. You might choose to let things like this go to make more space for playing and help you spend less time cleaning up.

Ask yourself when you used it or played with it last. Was it last week? Or has it been months? Remember, what takes up your space takes up your time (and I'm talking about more time *cleaning*), so choose carefully what to keep.

decisions, decisions

Still not sure if you should get rid of something? Can't remember how long it's been since you used or played with it? Let this list of questions help you decide:

- Is this one of your most favorite things in your room?
- Would you be able to give this item to someone who really needed it and feel happy about giving it away?
- Is it broken, or can it be used the way it is right now?
- How many times have you used it since your birthday last year? Is that number high enough that the item is worth keeping and cleaning regularly?

Clutter makes life harder. And if clutter is made up of the stuff in your room that you don't use or need, then you need to find and remove all the clutter in your space.

Now, you'll find some items in your room that you don't really care about but still need, like socks. Socks are something you use all the time, so even though they're not super special, keep your socks. It's not clutter if it's used.

By asking yourself how often you use something in your room, you're **being the boss of your space and your stuff.** A lot of people let clutter make all the rules and take over! They think that just because they own something now, they should always own it. But they don't stop and think about how all that stuff affects their life. And do you know what happens? They spend all their time taking care of stuff they don't really care about, instead of doing what they want to do. Isn't that crazy? We don't want to do that. We want to be in charge of our spaces.

3. In my dream room, is this object something I would want to play with or use?

Look at the picture of your dream room you drew in chapter 2. This question helps you play pretend in a way that helps you make smart decisions about what to keep and what to get rid of. Picture yourself in your room. It is exactly the way you

a note from Leland

HOW DO YOU KNOW WHAT TO GET RID OF AND WHAT TO KEEP?

Do you really play with that toy still? I used to think that I wanted to keep everything *just in case* I felt like playing with those things one day, but the fact is, I have to clean up *all the time* if I keep everything. So when you look at each of your toys, ask yourself, *Do I really play with that?* And if you earn your own money from doing chores or extra work around the house, ask yourself this: *If I worked for months to save up money, would I spend it on this toy again?* If you wouldn't, then maybe you don't really love it enough to keep it.

want it—your toys are all your favorites, cleaning your room is a breeze, schoolwork is so much faster, and your room looks really cool.

In this dream world, would you still play with this toy? Would you still read this book? Does this item help your room look and feel the way you want it to, or is it something you don't want to spend your time on?

This question can help you use your imagination to create a room that feels like your dream room.

What if I Feel Scared to Get Rid of Things?

Sometimes we're worried about getting rid of stuff, even if it's clutter. It's okay to feel that way. This is a change from what you've been doing, and that can be scary sometimes.

If you're nervous, just take it slow. It's okay to keep things because you're not sure. It's okay to skip the toys and start with something else. It's okay to read this whole book and learn the entire process before you start getting rid of clutter.

How do you feel about getting rid of stuff that isn't your favorite, no longer gets used, or just sits there, taking up space?

0	1	2	3	4	5	6	7	8	9	10

Totally not happy   Really happy

Think about what a jerk clutter has been in your room. It's been making you spend so much time cleaning up when you'd rather be playing. Or it's making you spend a long time on homework because your brain is too distracted by clutter to focus on schoolwork. It's been stealing your energy and making your brain sleepy. Clutter is not a nice friend!

Remembering what a problem clutter is can help you get excited about getting rid of things so you can live happier and smarter and better.

And remember, **every time you get rid of something, you are making more space for better things!** Things like happiness, new toys for your birthday, more play time, and more fun!

Won't I Hurt People's Feelings by Getting Rid of Presents They Gave Me?

It can be hard, even scary, to get rid of things that have been given to you by other people, especially people you love and see often. It's okay to feel this way, but don't let it stress you out. Let that stress go for a minute.

Imagine keeping every single thing anyone ever gives you. Every piece of paper, every birthday card, every toy, every blanket, every candy bar wrapper, *everything*.

Can you imagine how much space that would take up if you did that forever? Oh my goodness, all that stuff would take up *so much* space! You might even grow up and have to buy two houses just to store all the stuff! Or maybe you'd have to spend money renting someone's garage just for all the stuff your grandparents, friends, and other family members have given you. That would be really hard to keep organized. And you wouldn't have any space left for playing or resting.

And what would happen if you moved? Would you take *all* that stuff with you? That would be a lot of work! You would have so much stuff everywhere, it would take over your whole life!

Do you know what would actually happen? You'd probably never really be able to enjoy anything because there would be way too much stuff. If you wanted to find the teddy bear Grandma gave you, you would have to dig through piles and piles and *piles* of stuff in all your houses and all your garages. You might not ever find it!

When we treat every single thing like it is special, then nothing can be special. There's too much stuff, and we're acting like each item is equally important—and we know that's not true. The toy your uncle gave you two years ago that you never play with and completely forgot about is not as important as the big dollhouse or the skateboard your parents gave you that you play with every day. The stuff you use and love matters more.

Plus, if you kept everything, do you know how much time you'd have to spend picking up? **So much!** There'd be no time left to play, hang out with your friends, or do anything fun. That's not the point of having things. Wouldn't you rather have things that make you happy, that are worth picking up, and that don't suck up all your time and space?

Now that we've imagined that, do you see why it's important to keep your stuff pared down so that it's not overwhelming? It's normal to get rid of things, even things people give us as gifts. It's not mean, and it's not rude. It's necessary.

a note from Bella

When people give you presents, they're showing you that they love you. The present is just a symbol of their love, but it is not their love itself.

When you don't use something that somebody gave you, it becomes clutter. And we know how mean and nasty clutter is!

If someone loves you, they want your room to be a happy space, not a cluttered space. It's okay to get rid of it!

If people ask you what you would like for your birthday or a holiday celebration, you can give them a list of items you would really love. Think through your choices in advance so you're adding awesome things to your awesome space—and not future clutter.

You can also ask for gifts that won't take up space—like a membership to the zoo, a digital gift card to spend within a video game you like to play, a restaurant gift card, or just cash!

WHERE TO START

Okay, so we've tackled how to get rid of unused clutter. Now let's get started on actually decluttering it.

Toys

The best place to start is the toys. Go into your toy box or wherever your toys are kept and pick one up. Look at it and ask yourself the three helpful questions we talked about earlier in

Sometimes it helps to practice making decisions. So before you make some decisions about your own unused stuff, let's think about Liam's bedroom.

Liam loves to play his keyboard, build miniature robots using his engineering kit, and ride his bike. He hasn't worked on decluttering his room before, so his drawers and shelves are pretty stuffed. He wants more room to build his robots, so he starts to declutter his room.

Liam finds an old ball and glove that he used when he played T-ball. He loved playing T-ball with his friends when he was younger, but he doesn't play anymore. What advice would you give?

a. Keep the ball and glove. How else will Liam remember his T-ball days?

b. Keep the ball and get rid of the glove. Maybe he'll play with the T-ball again one day. Who knows?

c. Get rid of the ball and glove. He doesn't use them anymore, and someone else might love playing with them.

Then Liam picks up the book his uncle bought him two weeks ago: *The Beginner's Guide to Keyboards.* He hasn't used it yet because his keyboard is covered with LEGOs and dirty clothes. What advice would you give?

a. Throw it away. If Liam hasn't used it in the past two weeks, he never will.
b. Put it in the give-away pile. Liam can't play his keyboard with all that stuff on it.
c. Put it in the keep pile. Once Liam finishes decluttering and cleaning his room, he'll have more time and space to play his keyboard.

Finally, Liam looks at the big beanbag chair in the middle of his room. His older sister got it for him for Christmas last year, and he thought he was going to love it. But he can't really use it while building robots or playing his keyboard, and it takes up most of the floor space in his room. What advice would you give?

a. Keep it. He should never give away something he received as a gift.
b. Store it somewhere else, like in another room.
c. Give it to a friend or donate it to a thrift store. Liam's dream room includes space for building robots, and this beanbag chair is unused and in the way.

Now that you've decided what's best for Liam, let's figure out what's best for you, your space, and your unused stuff!

this chapter (also listed at the bottom of this page). Those questions are like your sidekick in your battle against clutter.

When you're finished making your keep and give-away piles of your toys, you can discuss your decisions with your grown-up and pack up all the toys in the give-away pile. Instead of throwing the toys away, take them to a donation center.

Donation centers collect people's unwanted things and give or sell them to other people who need or want them. What an awesome way to put your clutter to use to help others! What may be clutter and extra stuff to you could be a favorite toy to someone else.

tHRee QuestiONS tO aSK WHeN GettiNG Rid Of CLutteR

1. If this object went missing, would I notice and be really sad? Or would I not even notice because it's not important to me?
2. How often do I play with this or use it?
3. In my dream room, is this object something I would want to play with or use?

Clothes

Going through your clothes can be a lot easier if you go through them with a grown-up. So if you want to do this with a grown-up, go ahead. But if you want to do it on your own, let them know. And remember, I'm here to help you!

The first thing you want to do is go through your clothes and pull out anything that you don't wear because it is ripped or stained or damaged. Make a pile of those clothes and talk to your grown-up about the problem with them and why you don't wear them. Clothes that you're not wearing because there's something wrong with them shouldn't be kept in your drawers and closets. They're taking up space for no reason.

Next, you're going to pull out anything that doesn't fit or that you aren't sure fits. Try on your clothes one item at a time.

Your clothes should not be any of the following:

- Uncomfortably tight on your body
- Too loose or baggy
- Pinching, rubbing, or hurting you
- Keeping you from moving around and sitting comfortably

If there's a piece of clothing that you never put on because you don't like the way it fits you, no need to try it on—just put it in the give-away pile.

Next, you're going to pull out clothes you don't wear because you just don't like them. Sometimes a piece of clothing fits us and isn't damaged, but we never wear it because we just don't like it. This means that those clothes are not serving you. Clothes are supposed to be worn, make you feel comfortable, make you feel good, keep you warm, and keep you dressed. If a piece of clothing is not doing all those things, then it's not doing what it's made to do.

At this point your keep pile should be full of only things that fit you, that you like wearing, and that make you feel good. So take those clothes and fold them, hang them up, or organize them however you normally do. The most important thing is getting rid of the clothes that shouldn't be hanging around with you anymore.

Now show your pile of unused clothes to your grown-up and talk through the decisions you made. Then bag up whatever needs to be given away and take it to a donation center. Have a grown-up help you make phone calls to find out who will accept your clothes so they don't go to waste.

There are donation centers in almost every town. Some popular ones are Goodwill and the Salvation Army. You and a grown-up can take your things to a place like this if that works for you.

One of the best places to donate your undamaged clothes is a shelter. A lot of people go through really hard times and would appreciate some gently used clothing.

For damaged clothes, an animal shelter is the best place to take them. Animal shelters use clothes to clean the animals and to line the cages. Getting fabric is super helpful for them!

Donating your unused clothing can help people and animals, which can create positive feelings in you.

A NOTE FOR GROWN-UPS: Some thrift stores accept clothes and fabric in any condition so they can sell it by the pound and receive money for the nonprofit organization that they support.

When we give our unused stuff away, we get the chance to help people who are less fortunate than us. Imagine that a parent who has three kids goes into a place for help, and they get some gently used clothes. Some of those clothes used to be yours, and they fit one of the kids perfectly.

How does that make you feel? Write in the space below.

_____

_____

_____

_____

_____

Other Items

Now go through the rest of your stuff to see if you have any other unused items. Do you have sports equipment? Books? Hobby supplies, like stuff for painting, crafts, sewing, or photography?

As you go through each of the other items, think about whether these items would live in your dream room. Consider whether you actually spend time using these items. Then divide them into your keep and give-away piles.

Let's talk about Books

It's good to have books! Books can make you smarter, teach you about people who live differently from you, grow your mind, and help you learn new things.

But books stop helping you when they pile up on a shelf and aren't being used. Use this chart to help you decide which books to keep and which ones to get rid of.

If you've already read it and don't plan to read or use it again, give it away. If you haven't read it and don't plan to, give it away. Don't feel pressured to keep books you don't want!

> **Have you already read it?**
> ☐ Yes.   ☐ No.

> **Are you planning to read it?**
> ☐ Yes.   ☐ No.

> **Is it a book you'll want or need to look at again, like a dictionary or schoolbook?**
> ☐ Yes.   ☐ No.

Are you starting to feel a little bit lighter? Now that the trash is gone and the stuff you are not using, wearing, or playing with is gone, you are on the path to creating your own, unique space—that awesome room of your dreams.

STEP 5

SORt tHROUGH aRtWORK and PaPERS

part of life is dealing with paperwork. Papers come from everywhere—your school, your art, Sunday school, extra-curricular events, flyers, or notes from friends. It's a lot!

We want to make sure we stay on top of the papers that come into our space so that the papers don't pile up in each room.

One time, Leland's room got really messy, and he asked me for help with it. We started cleaning out his drawers, and he had so much paper in there, I couldn't believe it! He had coloring pages his brother had made for him, artwork he'd been working on but forgot to finish, flyers from school, homework scratch paper, and more. Papers were everywhere!

We don't want that to keep happening! So you need a plan for getting all the extra papers out of your space now and for managing the papers that will keep coming in.

ARTWORK

Artwork can be anything that you created, but usually it's a piece of paper with a drawing on it. Whatever it is that you like to create, those creations can easily take over your space. In our house, that has definitely happened because Bella and

Leland love to draw. I used to walk through my house and see artwork on the desk, on the counters, under their beds, and on the kitchen table. I'm surprised I didn't have artwork coming out of my ears!

You might have loads of art in your room, or you might have barely any at all. It all depends on your interests and how you use your time.

But if you have any amount of artwork or school papers in your room, you need to sort through it. Gather all the artwork you have in your room and put it in one big pile. Now you're going to sort the artwork using the super easy system Bella and I came up with when we first decluttered all the artwork in our house.

First, you need to sort the big pile of artwork into three smaller piles.

PILE 1: This pile is for the artwork that can be thrown away. If you don't have a trash can nearby, grab one now to make this step even easier.

PILE 2: This pile is for the art you want to remember. These are the creations you like but don't love.

PILE 3: This pile is for your masterpieces.

Now, here's the hard part—you actually have to look at each art piece and decide which pile it belongs in. But don't worry. I'm going to make the process as easy as possible for you.

Have you ever watched a YouTube video and then given it a rating? Or have you ever been on Amazon and seen a rating for a product? Have you ever rated your characters in your video game? Well, now you're going to look at your artwork and give it a rating based on how you feel about it. These ratings will help you make decisions.

Rating scale:

1: I Don't Really Care About This

2: I Like This

3: I Love This

Rating 1: I Don't Really Care About This

This rating is for these situations:

- If an art piece has just a couple of scribbles on it and you don't even remember what you were doing with it
- If you used a piece of paper for a quick sketch or to try out all the new colors in your marker set
- If you tried to create something you love, but you just don't like how it turned out

These types of artwork get a rating of 1 and should go in pile 1.

Rating 2: I Like This

This rating is for these situations:

- If you like your artwork, but it doesn't have that special something that makes you want to keep it on your wall or show all your friends
- If you worry that you'd regret throwing the artwork away, even though you know you don't want to display the artwork (at least not now)

These types of artwork get a rating of 2 and should go in pile 2.

Rating 3: I Love This

This rating is for these situations:

- If you consider your artwork a masterpiece—the very best of the best that you've created
- If you're super proud of your artwork and want to display it in your room or show it to family and friends
- If you'd be sad if you got rid of the artwork or if something were to spill on it and ruin it

These types of artwork get a rating of 3 and should go in pile 3.

When you're going through a big pile, it can feel really overwhelming. You might want to stop, change your mind, and give up. If it helps, before you start, find a way to make the sorting process more fun. Play some music, put on your favorite show, or ask a sibling, friend, or your grown-up to help you. You could also set a timer and challenge yourself to see how fast you can get through your pile.

Once everything is sorted into the three piles, you've got to do something with each pile.

Pile 1

The papers in pile 1 are pieces we don't care about keeping. So put everything in that pile in the recycle bin, and you're done!

Pile 2

We want to save all the artwork in pile 2, but we don't want it to take up space. So here's a simple solution: take a picture of each piece! You can do this with your phone or your grown-up's phone.

At our house, we use an app called the Scanner App. Have you ever seen an actual scanner? It's a machine that attaches to a computer like a printer. It can scan an image and send the data to the computer. Then you have a digital photo of the image! The Scanner App does the same thing, but it's way faster. Simply place the piece of art on a table or the floor, then take a picture of it using the Scanner App. Later, if you ever decide you want a physical copy of your artwork, you can just go to your digital file, print it out, and frame it. The printed version will look exactly the same as the original artwork. It will even be the same size!

Once you have scanned all of your art pieces from pile 2, you or your grown-up can organize all the photos you took into a digital folder. See if they can save the folder on your computer and make sure it's backed up on the cloud too. We label ours "Bella's Artwork" and "Leland's Artwork." That way, when we're looking through the photos again, we'll know who created what.

a note from Bella

I love to put on my headphones and listen to an audiobook while I sort through my artwork.

Now that a photo of each piece of artwork in pile 2 is saved, you can get rid of the actual pieces of paper. That's right! Throw them in the recycle bin. Or if you want to do something fun with the art, you can give it away! Our family does this a lot, and it's awesome! We put a drawing in a big envelope and write a kind note on the front. Usually the note says it's a gift for whoever finds it and needs to smile. Then we take the envelopes out on errands with us and leave them on public bulletin boards in coffee shops and stores.

Pile 3

Everything in pile 3 was rated 3, a masterpiece. So before we talk about what to do with these art pieces, go through the pile one more time and make sure that everything is a true masterpiece because these are the art pieces you're going to keep for now.

Remember, **what takes up your space takes up your time**. It's okay to have stuff, but just make sure that stuff is worth it. And now that you

have your final pile 3, you have one more decision to make: What do you want to do with these masterpieces?

Display the Masterpieces

At our house, we love to display the masterpieces. Sometimes we put them in frames. We have one wall in our house that's covered in the kids' artwork in white frames. Ask your grown-up if there's a space in your house where you could do something similar.

Sometimes we hang the masterpieces on the kitchen wall using washi tape. With this special type of tape, you can hang the art on the wall without ruining the paint. It's really easy to do this and costs less than hanging the art in frames.

Give Away the Masterpieces

Sometimes we give the masterpieces to grandparents. Bella has given her masterpieces to her grandmother to hang in her house. Her grandmother loves it, and Bella loves that her art

is being enjoyed and that she made someone happy by giving this gift. Her art is getting the attention it deserves.

Try It Out

Take one of your completed masterpieces or create a brand-new masterpiece this week. Then write a kind note and give the art piece and note to a family member. Taking the time to make something special for someone isn't just a nice gift for a loved one; it's also good for your heart!

Other Masterpiece Ideas

- Buy or decorate a binder or photo album. You can put your favorite art pieces in the plastic sleeves or scrapbooking pages. This can become its own work of art!
- Pick out a special box or container for only your favorite pieces. This could be a colorful accordion folder, a basket with a lid, a pretty box, or even something you customize and decorate yourself. Remember, this is not for everything. It's just for your masterpieces.
- Use a metal board, bulletin board, or other clipboard to create a special spot in your room that displays some of your favorite pieces.

Once you decide what to do with your masterpieces, you're done sorting through your artwork. Good job! Remember, if you don't have a plan, your artwork is going to keep piling up, and you'll have to do this again. We don't want that. We want a system that keeps working for you so it never becomes a giant pile again.

PAPERS

Let's talk about papers. Papers come in and out of the house all the time, and they can start to pile up worse than artwork! We get papers from a lot of places, but most of them come from school. To keep all those papers from turning into clutter, we've

Because I draw every day and I love art, it's a part of my week to sort through my creations. That way, my art never takes over the whole house again.

My mom and I have created a storage system for all of my artwork and a schedule for me to go through it. Here's my artwork system.

I have a magazine holder from Target that I keep on my desk, and every time I complete a piece of artwork, I put it in the magazine holder so it's all in one place. Once a week, I go through it and decide what is trash, what is a masterpiece, and what is something I just want to remember that I did. I even use the same 1–3 rating scale as we taught you earlier in this chapter. Once I'm finished sorting, I recycle everything with a rating of 1, I take a photo of everything with a rating of 2, and I display or give away everything with a rating of 3. It's that easy!

created a system for organizing them.

The most important thing you need is a special spot in your house for all your papers, a place that you and your grown-up can access quickly, since your grown-up usually needs to see the papers you bring home.

Where's the best place for *you* to put papers you bring home? In your room? On a table in a main area of your house? In a tray that sits on the kitchen counter? In a magazine holder on top of your grown-up's desk? Next to the mail drop-off spot in your home? Talk to your grown-up about it and brainstorm some solutions together.

Here are a few ideas:

- Have a dedicated space for putting paperwork that your grown-up needs to see.
- When you come home from school, put the important papers in that designated space before you put away your backpack.
- Have your grown-up set a calendar reminder for you to sort through paperwork together, talk about anything important that the paperwork addresses, and make decisions and plans as needed. (A great day to do this is on Sunday night, right before the new week starts!)

Write down your plan below.

_____

_____

_____

It might feel weird to think about managing papers. You're growing up, you have a space that's yours to keep clean, and you have schoolwork to do—but you're also still a kid.

Getting older has so many good things that come with it, but it also has some responsibilities that can be kind of tough.

And doing hard things is, well, *hard*. But if you don't do them, those things actually get *even harder* to deal with. A part of growing up is realizing that it's actually easier for *you* if you deal with hard things when you first come across them. Life will be so much easier if you can learn not to avoid responsibility but look at it as a good thing and decide to be the person who takes charge of your life.

When you do things like notice a problem with the papers in your room and come up with a solution, you take responsibility for your stuff and your life. This is something that not even all adults know how to do! So keep being an awesome action-taker!

And now that you've sorted through your artwork and papers, it's time to organize all the items you put in your keep pile.

find a place for what you're keeping

everything you own needs a place to live.

As you sort through your keep pile and put things away, look at each item and make sure it's something you use all the time or really love. This is how I'd like you to think about your possessions now as we go through the decluttering process, but it's also something you can do each time you clean your room in the future. Don't store things you don't need, want, use, or love. Your things should make you feel happy and be useful to you. For example, shoes you wear almost every day to school are useful. Your favorite toy is something that makes you happy. These things are not clutter.

But if you don't have enough space for the things that you're keeping, that's a problem we've got to fix.

So let's get started!

REVIEW YOUR SPACE

Your room is like a container for a big part of your life. Your room is where you live for several hours a day and where you keep all your stuff. It's where you're growing up. It's an important place, so you want to make sure it isn't stuffed with junk. And you want to make sure it uniquely reflects you.

Look around your room. Look at what you've decided to keep and, in the list below, check off each category of item that you have. Add any other types of items you may own.

MY KEEP LIST

- ☐ Shirts
- ☐ Sweaters
- ☐ Pants
- ☐ Dresses
- ☐ Jackets
- ☐ Shoes
- ☐ Socks
- ☐ Undergarments
- ☐ Pajamas
- ☐ Stuffed animals
- ☐ Toys I play with regularly
- ☐ Art supplies
- ☐ Artwork

- ☐ Coloring books and drawing pads
- ☐ School stuff
- ☐ Blank paper
- ☐ Notebooks
- ☐ Pens and pencils
- ☐ Books
- ☐ Hobby supplies
- ☐ _____
- ☐ _____
- ☐ _____

Does each category of stuff have a place to live in your room? For example, toys can go in a toy chest, books can go on shelves, and shoes can sit at the bottom of a closet. Try filling in the list below with homes for each category.

Shoes can live on the closet floor.

Books can live on the bookshelf by my bed.

_____ can live _____.

_____ can live _____.

_____ can live _____.

_____ can live _____.

_____ can live _____.

_____ can live _____.

_____ can live _____.

_____ can live _____.

_____ can live _____.

_____ can live _____.

_____ can live _____.

_____ can live _____.

If you can't find a home for some of your things, you may need to go back through all the stuff in your room and reevaluate what you're keeping. Sometimes we decide to keep too much, and we don't have enough space in our room to hold it all. If the space where you decide to keep something is overflowing, you probably have too much.

And you may need to discuss with your grown-up about what you need to stay organized. Do you need a bin or chest for toys? A couple of bookshelves?

For example, we have a toy bin in the bonus room at our house. If the bin gets full, the kids know it's time to get rid of some toys.

You only have so much space! You've got to work with what you've got and make sure your room is clutter-free and helping you feel creative and happy.

What parts of your room are overstuffed? Take this book with you and look at those overstuffed spots. What can you get rid of?

Now put everything you listed in a pile.

How do you feel when you think of getting rid of some of your things? Are you happy, sad, nervous, or something else? Why do you think you feel that way?

_____

_____

Feelings are normal, and they are helpful. They show us what is going on inside of us—the things we can't see.

How do you feel about giving away your things to someone who might really need them?

_____

_____

It is okay to feel anxious. It is okay to feel happy. It is okay to feel whatever you are feeling. It is also okay for your feelings to change a whole bunch! Getting rid of clutter brings up lots of feelings in adults too.

The most important thing for you to do when you feel feelings is to write them down. This makes it so much easier for you to understand your feelings. Feelings just want to be noticed. Feeling them, talking about them, and writing them down helps them be noticed.

Use this space to notice any feelings you have while reading the rest of this book.

_____

_____

_____

_____

Now that you've made some decisions and connected to your feelings about this process so far, let's take some more action.

For the items you've decided to give away, bag them up and ask your grown-up to donate them. For the items you've decided not to keep, throw them away or recycle them. For the items you've chosen to keep, put them back in their place or find a new place for them that will work better.

You're doing great!

ORGANIZE YOUR STUFF

Each item you own needs its own space and a method for staying organized. After all, if you don't have a plan for your things, your stuff will start to take over your room and get really messy. You're the boss of your stuff and your space, and thinking through how you will store and organize your stuff is the best way to keep stuff from becoming the boss of you.

Toys

Before you can organize your toys, you first need a list of all
the kinds of toys you have. Use the checklist below to help you.
Check the box next to all the toys you have.

☐ Action figures   ☐ Stuffed animals

☐ Board games and puzzles   ☐ Trucks

☐ Dolls

☐ Dress-up clothes and   ☐ _____

    costumes

☐ LEGOs   ☐ _____

☐ Plastic animals

☐ Race cars   ☐ _____

     ☐ _____

Look over your list of toys. What kind of storage do you have for toys? Is your space working for the kinds of toys that you're keeping? Why or why not?

_____

_____

_____

_____

_____

Pro Tip

If you own LEGOs, listen up! I have a special tip for you: don't store them with all your other toys. LEGOs can get messy quickly; they need their own space. Otherwise, they just get mixed in with all your other toys, and when you pull out your favorite monster truck, LEGOs fly everywhere!

Even just a small bin with enough space to store your LEGOs will work fine. It doesn't have to be fancy. But keeping LEGOs separate from other toys will make sure you don't lose any of the pieces. After all, nobody wants their LEGO set to be incomplete!

Clothes

Do you hang your clothes up, or do you fold them into dresser drawers or bins? Maybe you hang up some things and fold others.

I like hanging up all my clothes because it's easier for me to maintain. Bella likes to have her clothes in drawers because it takes less time for her to put them away.

One thing that's helped save space, especially when my kids have shared a room, is rolling clothes. For your shirts, shorts, and pants, lay them flat on the floor, fold them in half once, and

then just roll them. You can stack your rolled clothes in your drawers and fit a lot more in each one. If you share a dresser with a sibling or you have a lot of clothes, rolling your clothes this way will work really well for you!

a note from Leland

Even though I share a room with my little brother, I like that I have my own bin for my toys. It gives me privacy.

And I like how easy it is for me to find the toys I'm looking for because I don't have tons and tons of toys to sort through.

I *love* LEGOs! I organize them by color so I can easily find any piece I'm looking for. I also have a big table next to my LEGOs that's big enough for me to build any set I want on it. I like having space to create and build, and I have that space because I keep my LEGOs organized. They're easy to find and put away.

If you live somewhere that gets really cold, you're going to have more clothes than people who live in warmer climates, and you're also going to have bulkier items, like big coats. Try hanging your coats in your closet. (Stuffing them in a drawer never works!) Or if you use cold-weather items only a few times a year, store them in a bin that slides under your bed.

Think about your current system for taking care of your clothes. Do you take the time to hang up clothes? Do you prefer to fold them and store them in dresser drawers?

Is your system messy, or does it take you too long to put clothes away? If so, what new system will you try?

_____

_____

While we're on this topic, what's your system for dirty clothes?

Look around your room and take note of where your dirty clothes normally land. That is where you need to put a hamper.

If you already have a hamper in your room, but clothes are always piled on your floor near the bathroom door, your hamper is not working well for you! Move it to where you tend to drop your dirty clothes. If you don't have a hamper in your room, talk to your grown-up about getting one.

Activity and Sporting Equipment

Do you play any sports or go to any after-school activities? If you do, you probably own the gear that comes with it. For example, horseback riding lessons require special boots, and playing baseball means you have a bat, ball, and glove to practice with at home.

So where are you storing your gear? Is it in your room? Do you have enough space for it there, or is there another place in your home that could fit it better, like the garage?

In our house, we have baseball players, and we have a spot for them to take off their cleats and dump their gear in the garage. There's a bin for cleats, a laundry hamper for dirty socks and muddy uniforms, and hooks on the wall for their equipment bags. We always know where their baseball stuff is, mud doesn't get tracked in the house, and there's never any confusion about where to find their bags before practice.

What sports or activities do you participate in?

_____

_____

What gear or supplies do you own? Where are you currently storing that stuff?

_____

_____

Is that storage space working for you, meaning that everything can be put away easily and fits within your space? Or do you need to come up with a new system?

_____

_____

Take action! Move things around and talk to your grown-up about anything you might need help with.

Hobby Supplies

Do you have a hobby? If so, what supplies do you use?

_____

_____

If your hobby supplies are best kept in your room, where are you going to keep them? If they need to be placed in another space, what options do you have?

_____

_____

School Stuff

Organizing school stuff can be hard because you usually have to keep a lot of papers and supplies you don't _want_ to but _need_ to, at least until the school year ends. So to make the school stuff easier, you'll need a system for how to handle it.

Do you already have a system for the things that you use for school, including papers, homework, and your backpack? Maybe you have a paper tray to put paperwork your grown-up needs to see (like we talked about in chapter 5). Or you have a hook to hang your backpack.

Let's get super clear on your habits surrounding your school stuff so we can figure out the best system for you to set up in your room.

Where do you do homework?

_____

How long do you normally spend doing homework or studying per week?

_____

Where do you usually put your backpack when you come home?

_____

Where do you usually put papers that you bring home from school?

_____

Are there any problems with these habits? Sometimes when habits are not helpful, your grown-up might tell you that what you're doing isn't working well. Other times, you might be able to tell a habit is not helpful because you can never find your things when you need them.

Is there something you could change to make things easier?

_____

_____

Your Desk

If you have a desk in your room, you may have noticed that it can get *so* messy *so* quickly. You might not know what to keep or get rid of. Even if you do know what you want to keep, it can be tricky to keep all your desk stuff organized every day.

If you have a desk in your room, what do you use it for? Do you do your homework there? Do you draw there? Are you being creative there? Or do you not really use it at all? Or worse, is stuff just piling up on it?

_____

_____

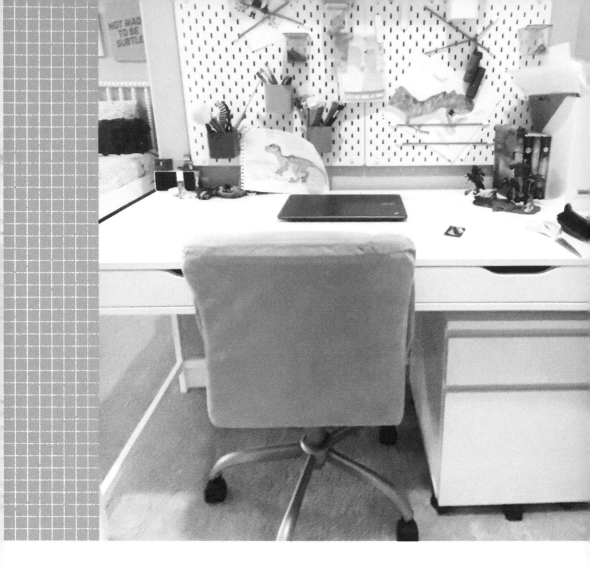

Based on your answer to those questions, let's get your desk
organized. If you're creative and using your desk to make art
and draw, then you're going to need trays or drawers to organize your art supplies and paper. You're also going to need a
place to store your art when you're done (like we talked about
in chapter 5).

If you use your desk to do homework and study, then you

want to make sure that the surface of the desk is cleared of any clutter. Pencils, erasers, and highlighters should be within reach so you don't have to go digging each time you need one. And if your grown-up lets you eat and drink in your room, make space for a coaster or a fun treat.

Think about how you use this desk and what you need to support you. How can you organize it? What can you add to make this place an area that feels good for you and supports you?

_____

_____

Books

Books are tricky because they can easily get overwhelming. This is an area where I have a hard time keeping things simple because I love to read. It's way too easy for me to end up with *tons* of books! But here's the thing: if you have already read a book and you won't want to read it again, there's really no point in keeping it.

Look at the books you've decided to keep and make sure that you truly want to keep them all. Now, look at the space you have to store them.

Do you have enough space? If not, you may need to pare down even more or figure out a new way to store your books, which we'll cover in the next chapter.

Pro Tip

An easy way to create more space for books without taking up space in your room is by using floating shelves on your wall, which your grown-up can help you find and install.

Random Stuff

As you're going through your room, you'll probably find some things that are yours but don't actually belong in your room. Things like your hairbrush (which should probably go in the bathroom) or the blanket used for snuggling on the couch (which should go back to the room with the couch in it) just need to be put away. We want your room to be clean, clear, and only for *your* things that you use in *your* room.

Okay, friend! Now that you've found a place for the things you're keeping, it's time to straighten up the details.

Make your bed, make sure nothing is on the floor, clean under your bed, and put things where they belong.

Done and done! Good job!

STEP 7

desiGn
your Space

Congratulations! Clutter isn't taking over your room anymore, and you're becoming the boss of your stuff.

Great work!

And now that you have systems in place so clutter can't take over again, it's time to make your space look how you want it to look.

This is one of the best parts of the whole process. This is where you get to dream and imagine really fun ways to make your room look a certain way—a way that fits your personality. It's the **creating** and **decorating** part after the decluttering part is done. Decluttering is truly wonderful, but the point is not that we all live in plain, empty rooms—it's to create a place that you love, that you can have fun in, that inspires you, that helps you rest, and that gives you space to grow. So let's get creating!

Go back to chapter 2 and look at the drawing you made of your dream room and the words you used to describe it. Do you still want your room to look and feel this way? Draw an updated picture of how you want your room to feel now that you've learned so much about decluttering (and yourself!) in these past few chapters.

Look closely at your drawing and then at your room. Does your room look more like your drawing now that you've removed the clutter? What do you need to do to make your room look and feel like your dream-room drawing?

_____

_____

_____

_____

For this step, talk to your grown-up. Everyone's house and family is different, so your grown-up may want to help you design your room right away, they may want to do a little bit now and more later, or they may want you to wait on all your plans for a while. That's between you and your grown-up, and it will be important to sit down and discuss budget, timelines, and possibilities.

For now, I'm going to give you some awesome ideas for designing your room.

Ready? Let's go!

DEFINING YOUR STYLE

Before you start designing your room, you need to know what your favorite design style is.

BOHEMIAN: This style uses blanket layers, rug layers, beads, textures, and colorful curtains. It's a bright, colorful, and busy style.

MINIMALIST: This style has clean lines, straight edges, and no layers. It's as simple as it can be and feels open and clean.

RUSTIC/FARMHOUSE: This style uses things that look old, are old and used, or are vintage. It also uses a lot of wood and metal pipes.

ECLECTIC: This style is unique because you can mix different styles! It's a very free style, so you have a lot more wiggle room in terms of design. There are fewer design rules for this style.

Which one of these design styles feels the best to you? Look at the pictures on pages 108–109. Which style do you like the most?

_____

Each of these styles can have a range of colors. Do you prefer the bright, airy, and light look, or the bold, dark, and moody look? Or somewhere in between?

_____

FIND YOUR FAVORITE STYLE

BOHEMIAN

RUSTIC/FARMHOUSE

MINIMALIST

ECLECTIC

CREATING A PLAN FOR YOUR DREAM ROOM

Creating a dream room requires careful planning. It's not about putting every single thing you love on your walls, dresser, and floor. It's about making decisions that follow your favorite design style and support the feeling you want in your room. So before you throw a decorating party and go a little crazy, let's go over some of the bigger changes you could make to transform your room.

Paint

Paint is the biggest change you can make to any room. The color on your walls creates the vibe you feel when you walk into your room.

For example, Bella's room has bright white trim and the walls are a very pale gray. It's very airy, bright, and happy.

In our old house, the walls in Bella's room were pink. It totally changed the vibe of her room. It was still happy and cute, but it was definitely less peaceful. The pink didn't make it easy to calm down, unwind, and go to sleep because the color felt loud.

If you don't like your room, changing the paint is a great place to start.

CHOOSING THE RIGHT COLOR

Each color creates its own vibe in a space. Look at this list of colors and their descriptions to see which colors you connect with.

BLUE: calming, cool
YELLOW: happy, inspirational, summery
PURPLE: royal, luxurious, creative
RED: confident, exciting, energetic
GREEN: relaxing, harmonious, lively
PINK: feminine, romantic, tranquil
BROWN: secure, content, comforting
ORANGE: warm, vibrant, enthusiastic
SILVER/GRAY: calming, cooling, luxurious
WHITE: young, cool, clean, fresh
BLACK: elegant, sophisticated, mysterious[1]

Which colors are you drawn to?

_____

_____

Out of the colors and feelings listed above, which ones would you like in your space?

_____

_____

Furniture

Furniture is a lot like paint in that one piece changes the way a room feels, and your furniture is a great way to express your style.

You may not need to change any of the furniture in your space. It might work just fine as it is! But if it is worn out or it doesn't match how you want your room to feel, changing it will make a huge difference.

Pro Tip

Remember, changing the style and feel of your room is not an excuse for bringing new clutter in! Make sure that as you and your grown-up are choosing what to have in your space, you are practicing your new skills. Do you really love each item? Do you need it? Is it going to serve a purpose or just sit around?

If you want your room to feel really soft, open, airy, and peaceful but you have all black furniture, switch to white pieces.

If you want a room that feels bolder or darker, switch white pieces to navy, black, or wood pieces.

If you want a room to feel happy and bright, bring colorful furniture pieces into it.

The good news is that buying new stuff is not the only way to change your furniture. You can take the pieces of furniture already in your room and change the way they look with the help of a grown-up.

add COLOR to WHat you've Got

Remember how paint changes the look of a room? Paint can also change the look of furniture. If you have a dresser that's dark wood that you want to be white, you could paint it. You could even order new knobs and legs to make it look like a whole new dresser.

You could paint your desk chair or a wooden bed frame. Almost anything can be painted—even metal furniture can be spray-painted. This is a fun, affordable way to make something look brand new without spending a ton of money and without wasting something that's in great shape.

Bedding

The easiest way to bring a fresh look into your room is to change the bedding.

Do you like your current bedding? Does it fit your personality? Is it snuggly enough? Or is it a few years old and has a character on it from a show that you don't watch anymore? You can shop online with a grown-up and find something that fits your age and style.

Choosing what's on your bed is super fun because it makes the whole space change! My bed is my favorite part of my room, other than my art. My mom and I chose a cozy white comforter, some bohemian throw pillows, and my three favorite stuffed animals, which sit in front of the pillows. Every day when I walk into my room, I smile.

tips for sharing a room

At some point, all four of my kids have shared a room with a sibling. If you share your room with someone, don't worry—you can still have your own style, enjoy your space, and also be a great roommate.

Here are some fun ideas to make sharing your room even more awesome:

- Divide the room down the middle with a long ribbon on the floor. Then you can each choose a theme color for your side of the room. Instead of sharing one room, the two different colors will make it feel like you each have your own smaller room.
- Have your grown-up get a room divider to give each of you more privacy. (That is, if you want more privacy. Some people like being able to see and talk to their roommate whenever they want, and that's great!)

- You and your roommate can choose the main color of the room together, then paint your furniture in your individual colors. If you share a dresser, you might even want to draw a line down the middle and paint one half your color and the other half your roommate's color.

It's super fun to get creative and make the space work for both of you.

Dresser and Desk

If you want to add some personality to your dresser or desk, make a few simple changes to really bring out your style and the vibe you want in your room. You can change the hardware by finding knobs or bar pulls that add some flair or interest to your furniture piece. Or you could change the look of the dresser and desk using paint and stencils. You can even use stick-and-peel wallpaper to add color and style in a few easy steps!

Storage

Without proper storage, your stuff will end up in messy piles. But there's a simple way to make sure you put each item back where it belongs: use storage that you think looks good and makes you happy!

Let's talk about a few items that always need good storage.

BOOKS

One thing that can take up a lot of space and be tough to organize is books. A great place to start with designing your space

is getting a new bookshelf or bookcase to hold your books in a way that looks good.

Bella has bookshelves on her wall so that they're off the floor. I have a bookcase on the wall with drawers so you can't see what's inside. You and your grown-up can decide what works for you and your space.

Books can also be decorations. If you have a table next to your bed, putting a few books stacked on top of each other can count as a decoration.

If you have open shelving, you may need bookends to keep the books from falling off the shelf. This is an opportunity to show your style in decorating your room.

Bella uses geodes (rocks that are filled with crystals) for bookends because she's super into rocks and crystals.

Leland has bookends that are chunks of wood carved into the shape of mountains. He found them in a store and really liked them.

Think of something you like that is sturdy enough to be a bookend, then use the bookends to show off your personal style.

TOYS AND ART SUPPLIES

In the dream room you've imagined, where do your toys live? Are they stored in a chest? Do you have a few favorite pieces on display, or do you put everything in containers so that your room feels spacious?

Are your art supplies tucked into a desk drawer? Or do you prefer to keep them in the playroom?

Choose storage pieces that will make it easy for you to put away your toys and art supplies when you're finished using them and will also make you smile when you see them. The goal is to make your room functional *and* fun!

ACCESSORIES

Do you own jewelry? Do you have video game accessories? Do you have cables and cases for your gadgets? If you have anything that comes with extras, then you're going to need a place to keep them.

Think through what would work best for your stuff and your space. If you need a basket or bin, find one that fits your favorite design style, the room colors you chose, and your personality.

Maybe you want a woven basket with handles that makes everything inside easy to access. Or maybe you'd like a storage bin with a lid so that you don't have to see the stuff inside unless you want to. You might even get a cardboard box and your art supplies and decorate it yourself to make a unique-to-you storage piece!

Decorations

This might be my favorite part of designing a dream room. When adding decorations to your room, you can let your imagination run wild! Almost anything you love can be represented in a decoration.

But remember, only let your most favorite things in your room. Decorations that you don't love will become clutter. And any decoration that keeps you from being able to use a part of your room (like a plant on your desk that takes up half your workspace) is not worth it.

Plants

One of the easiest ways to make your room brighter and happier and make it match your style is by using plants.

Plants actually help you breathe in clean air when you're inside, and they make the space feel so much brighter. We have plants in almost every room, so our house kind of feels like a jungle, which is extra fun for our cat, Pico.

Plants are also living things, so they can help you learn responsibility because you have to take care of them, making sure they get the water and sunlight they need. Because plants are alive, they're like friends that hang out in your room all day. Plants are super special.

Leland picked out a tree to go in the corner of his room. It's a yucca tree, which is super easy to take care of and looks really cool. He uses a water meter to check the tree's water level so he knows when to water it again. He's really enjoyed having something to take care of that is his own and makes his room brighter.

Bella really likes cacti. She has a bunch in her room on her desk and shelves. She loves how tiny and cute they are.

If you want to try having a plant of your own, here are some that are easy to take care of:

- Air plants
- Boston fern
- Croton
- Dracaena
- Ponytail palm
- Pothos
- Rubber tree
- Snake plant
- Spider plant (It's not as creepy as it sounds!)
- Yucca tree
- ZZ plant

Things You've Made

You already know that Bella is an artist, but did you know that art is a big part of how she decorates her room?

Not only does she have art by other artists that she loves and is inspired by, but she has a wall in her room where she displays her own works of art.

Things You Love

Okay, so "things you love" isn't really specific, but that's a good thing! This is your chance to think of what makes you the happiest and find a way to represent those things in your room.

What do you love?

Examples: *Adventures, animals, cars, food, traveling, nature, sports, science, space, bright colors, books, or photography.*

_____

_____

_____

How do you want to incorporate what you love into your dream room? (Make sure it fits with your design style and color palette too!)

Examples: *Posters, artwork, framed photos, novelty items displayed on shelves, or figurines in the corner of your room.*

_____

_____

_____

Now talk with your grown-up about your plan for your dream room. Then work on making your room as fun and functional as it can be!

Maintain youR neW ROOM

You've done a lot of work to get clutter out of your way, so the last thing we want is for it to take over again. Because, remember, what takes up your space takes up your time.

The way you're going to keep winning the battle against clutter is by becoming the editor of your room.

BEING A GOOD EDITOR

You are the boss of your stuff, and to make sure that stuff never becomes the boss of you, you have to keep editing your room. To be the editor of something means that you're guarding it and making decisions about what comes in and what stays out. This is what you're going to do with your room from now on.

Because you've gotten rid of everything you don't need and don't love and because you've chosen a home for each item you kept, you won't have to clean your room as often, and when you *do* clean, it will hardly take any time at all.

But there is one new step you need to add to your cleaning routine. Don't worry—it doesn't take long, and you know how to do it! When you clean, look for what you could edit out of your room. You might see some items you kept during the decluttering process that you now realize you don't want or need anymore. Take those items out of your room. If they're in good shape, donate them. If they're broken or can't be used by anyone else, recycle them (if you can) or throw them away.

It also helps to declutter your room at specific times during the year.

Let's face it—things are coming into our lives all the time. Toys from the drive-thru, gifts from people, papers from school, artwork you create. It's constant! So a few times a year, we need to sort through our rooms and clear the clutter just like we did throughout this book.

You can set reminders for yourself to do this. The easiest way is to attach this decluttering process to a specific time of year. You probably get presents for your birthday and during the holidays, right? So you could plan to declutter your room around those times. For example, every year, the week before your birthday, you could sort through your things and declutter. Or every year, the week after the holidays, you could declutter your room. At the beginning and end of the school year is another great time to get ready for a fresh, new season of life by taking care of old clutter.

Do you have your own calendar? If so, make a reminder or ask your grown-up to put reminders on their calendars. An alert to do this every year during these times is a great way to start a lifelong habit of being the boss of your stuff and not letting it pile up and control you. You'll start a cycle of editing, decluttering, and repeating—this will help you be and stay the boss of your stuff.

What times of year make sense for you to do a check-in on your room and how much stuff is in it?

What's your plan to remember the check-in? Are you going to put it on your calendar? Can a grown-up put it in their phone as a reminder?

_____

_____

RESETTING YOUR ROOM

Now that you have your new space situated with a fresh look and your stuff is cleared out and organized, let's talk about keeping it that way!

I'm sure the last thing you want to have happen, after working so hard to create the space you want, is for your room to become messy all over again.

Think about how good it feels to have your room clear of clutter, organized, clean, and ready for you to enjoy.

Can you remember how it felt before you made these changes? Remember how it felt to walk into a cluttered, chaotic, stressful room? Remember how it felt to always be searching for a missing shoe or toy? Remember how it felt to be trying to focus on schoolwork with mess all around you? Let's not go back there!

Earlier we talked about helpful and unhelpful habits. Let's set up some helpful habits that will support you in keeping your room a space you enjoy being in.

Every day, your room needs a small reset. Picking things up off the floor, putting misplaced items away, clearing off the tops of your dresser, desk, and tables, throwing out trash—all these things help to reset your space.

Every week, your room needs a slightly bigger reset. Taking out the trash, organizing your dresser and desk drawers, taking the sheets off your bed to be washed—these tasks help give your room a bigger reset before you start a new week.

How can you remind yourself to reset your room at the end of each day and week? Can you put a Post-It note on your bathroom mirror? Or set an alarm?

Most people need a reminder to help them complete a new task. It takes thirty days of reminders before doing that task becomes a habit. But once it's a habit, you won't need a reminder anymore!

a Race to Reset!

How long do you want to spend resetting your room? Less than ten minutes? Less than five?

The next time you need to reset your room, set a timer for ten minutes and race to get your room reset in that time. If you can't do it in time, you might need to declutter your room some more. Then the next day, set the timer for five minutes and reset the room as fast as you can.

Continue editing your room and decluttering until you're happy with how long it takes you to reset your room.

REMINDER: Don't stress! Your room does not need to be perfect. It doesn't always need to be clean. That's not the point of what we're doing here. Your room is a space that is meant to support *you*. You do not need to be stressing out about always keeping it perfect.

BECOMING A MINIMALIST

What is a minimalist? To me, it means decluttering and keeping only the items I use and really love. It's not about following rules. It's thinking about what comes into your space and asking if it's worth it. Most people just let new items come into their space without thinking about it, but soon the stuff stacks up and up and up until it takes over their space.

Decluttering and maintaining your room may seem hard at first, but there's something about this process that not everyone knows. It actually makes your life easier! People who finish this process are happier, they have more time for what they want to do, and they enjoy being in their space more than most people. And that's what I want for you! You'll understand that there's more to life than stuff. And that's what this is all about—living a good life, instead of letting stuff take up all your time and energy.

STEP 9

Buy thoughtfully

as you grow up, you'll have different wants and needs, and you'll discover new interests. At the same time, your room and your stuff will need to change to match your current stage of life. And that's natural! One of the most important skills to learn along the way—and a great way to stay the boss of your stuff—is to buy things thoughtfully.

Because you're a kid, grown-ups buy most of your stuff for you, but a lot of grown-ups haven't learned the lessons that you're learning in this book. You might receive a lot of stuff that you don't want or need, which becomes clutter. Just remember that you're in charge of your space, and it's okay to donate something to people in need if that thing isn't worth your time or space.

BUY ONLY WHAT YOU REALLY WANT AND NEED

Most people buy stuff without even thinking about it, but I want to encourage you to do something different—to think carefully before purchasing something. For example, if you grow out of your clothes and need to buy more, look for clothes that are a good value:

- They fit well.
- They look good on you.
- They're versatile, which means you could make a lot of outfits with them.
- They won't wear out easily.
- They're a fair price.

When you're the boss of your stuff, you think differently about making purchases. After all, you took all that time to declutter your closet and dresser, and you don't want to undo it by spending recklessly on clothes you won't like in two months. You know that if you don't really *love* the red shirt you just bought, you won't wear it, and it'll just get stuffed in a drawer—until one day when you'll realize it doesn't even fit anymore. That red shirt becomes a waste of money and space. Saving your money for something you truly *love* will make you and your space much happier.

So how do you know when to buy something? Use this list of questions to help you decide:

- Do I need this?
- Do I love this enough for it to take up space in my room?
- Even if all my friends told me they didn't like the item, would I still love it and use it regularly?
- Do I love this enough to take care of it, knowing that adding another item to my space will make cleaning my room take longer?
- How often will I use this?

Buying only what you really want and need is tricky, especially because the act of purchasing can be fun. Sometimes you may feel excited about buying something, but the excitement is more about the thrill of getting something new than anything else. But when the excitement wears off, you're stuck owning something that you don't care much about. It just takes up space in your room, and then you want to buy something else to feel that same excitement again.

Everyone can get stuck in that buying loop, and it always ends the same way: an empty piggy bank and a room full of stuff you don't use. But don't worry—there's a simple solution! When you feel the urge to buy something, go home and think about it for a max of three days. It's helpful to give yourself a time limit! You might even talk to your grown-up about the pros and cons of buying the item. If you still really want to buy the item in a few days and you know it's a good decision for you and your space, go back to the store and buy it.

Thoughtful buying is about thinking deeply and being careful with what you buy. It's caring about your space more than caring about having lots of stuff.

BUY FROM GOOD COMPANIES

Thoughtful buyers also carefully choose the stores they buy from. They might consider what the company's values are, how the company treats their workers, what materials are used to create the products, and what effect the company is having on the world.

For example, some companies give a pair of shoes away to someone in need for every pair of shoes they sell. That's a cool company to buy shoes from because they're making a positive difference in the world every day! Think about it: if you need a new pair of shoes anyway, buying from a company that gives a pair of shoes away with each purchase is a more thoughtful purchase. You and your grown-up are using your money to help someone at the same time as getting the shoes you need. This is thoughtful buying.

There's a lot to consider when making a purchase, but being a thoughtful buyer is about pausing and thinking before actually buying. The next time you need to buy something, consider these questions first:

it's a PROCESS

It's good to remember that we are all learning, and we all make mistakes. Sometimes we buy things that we end up really loving and using well. But sometimes we buy things we really thought we were going to love, but then it turns out that we don't. Don't beat yourself up—just commit to growing, asking good questions, and learning from your experiences.

- Is this a company I really want to support?
- What is this product made out of? Are the materials helping or hurting the earth?
- Were any animals harmed when they made this product?
- Is this company known for treating their workers well?

Write down the lists of questions from this chapter on a piece of paper and carry it with you—or if you have a phone, take a picture of these questions—and review them while you're shopping. Each question will help you make wise buying decisions and help you stay **the boss of your stuff**.

Buy thoughtfully IRL

Now that you've learned how to buy thoughtfully, try it out! Before you make a purchase, fill out this form to see if it's a good decision for you and your space.

Do I need this item? If so, why?

_____

_____

Do I love this enough for it to take up space in my room?

_____

_____

Even if all my friends told me they didn't like the item, would I still love it and use it regularly?

_____

_____

Do I love this enough to take care of it, knowing that adding another item to my space will make cleaning my room take longer?

_____

_____

How often will I use this?

_____

_____

What are the pros and cons of owning this?

_____

_____

Do I want to support this company?

_____

_____

Other thoughts to consider:

_____

_____

_____

_____

instead of stuff

Sometimes we have to buy stuff. We all need pants, right? But when it comes to gifts, you might enjoy giving and receiving experiences more than stuff. Here are a few ideas:

- Instead of a present, what about a day at the zoo, museum, or amusement park? Fun memories with family and friends are worth so much more than physical things!
- Rather than adding to your art supply stash, what about a painting class? You can learn new skills and learn how to use the supplies you may already have.
- Do you love sports or music? Tickets to a concert or favorite team's game is another way to share the gift of experience.

What ideas do you have?

- _____

- _____

Learning how to be a thoughtful buyer of things is a wonderful skill that will help you for your entire life—and learning how to value people and experiences over stuff will make your life far richer than any birthday or Christmas present you could hope to get.

CHANGE YOUR ROOM, CHANGE YOUR LIFE

How you are with one thing is how you are with everything. This is something I say a lot. I have found it to be so true! It means that how you choose to act in one part of your life will affect how you act in the other parts. For example, if your room is a crazy mess all the time, then you're probably messy at school too—you keep losing your pencils, your backpack is always messy, and you forget important things a lot.

A lot of people hear this and get really stressed out. They think it's a bad thing that all our actions are connected. They think it makes life harder. But I actually think it's a good thing. We can use this knowledge to make life easier and better for us. Because if how you are with one thing is how you are with everything, then you can make your whole life easier, better, and different just by changing one thing. Pretty cool!

If you can change your whole life by changing one part of it, then the easiest thing to change first is your physical space, which is perfect because we've already done that!

It's a lot easier to declutter and clean your room than to figure out why you're disorganized at school. And once your space is less messy, you'll have an easier time remembering where your pencils are, and your brain will have more room to remember important things, like getting that science fair project finished by the end of the month. That one decision—to clean your room—will keep making your life better. Doing one positive thing will motivate you to do something else good. In fact, when you change your room, you change your life. You'll feel better about yourself, and you'll have more time for what you really care about.

PICK YOUR WORD

If how you are with one thing is how you are with everything, how do you want everything to be? What is one word you want to embody in your life? Pick your word, write it down in big letters on a piece of paper, and hang it on your wall so you will be reminded every day what you're wanting to put out into the world and how you want to live.

Here are some example words:

Hopeful   Joyful   Positive

Gentle   Kind   Respectful

SHOWING YOURSELF RESPECT

If you were to start caring about how your room feels because you care about yourself, then that care is going to echo in other parts of your life and other parts of your day. It's really all about respecting yourself and your space.

Respect means thinking highly of someone because that person is amazing. Respect is also a way to show you care.

Do you have respect for yourself? How do you show yourself respect or disrespect?

Which do you think is an act of respecting yourself: leaving your stuff all over the floor and bed, or picking up your room and giving yourself a clean space and more space in your brain to focus on other things? Why?

_____

_____

_____

_____

a note from Bella

I tend to be creative and messy. I used to think that was a bad thing—to be messy—but my mom helped me see that it's actually good to be messy in some areas, like art, which I love! But I respect myself enough to not live in a mess. I can use my tendency toward messiness in ways that make me a better artist, but I can respect myself and my space at the same time. What tendencies can you balance with self-respect?

When I get a little lazy and don't pick up my room before I go to sleep, I wake up the next morning to a mess. It puts me in a bad mood right away, and that makes sense because I'm not showing myself respect! But we can choose to respect ourselves every day, and one way we do that is by caring for ourselves, which boosts our mood and our self-esteem!

Write down some things that you love about yourself.

Examples: *My eyes, my kind heart, or my awesome math skills.*

_____

_____

These things make you, *you*. They make you awesome. You are so worthy of love and respect from yourself and others!

If we think about how awesome we are and how much we respect and love ourselves as we pick up our rooms, get our backpacks ready for school, and choose snacks, then everything changes because we *feel* different and are *doing things* differently! Look at how much good is happening just because you changed your room.

You are very special, my friend. You deserve a room that is clean and tidy and works for you. You deserve **respect** and **love** from yourself and from others.

Repeat these sentences as often as you want. If you did this every day for a month, imagine how different you'd feel!

I deeply and completely love and accept myself.
I'm worthy of good things.
I respect myself and the way that I do things.
I choose to do my best.

MAKING SPACE FOR WHAT YOU LOVE

You've created so much space for your brain to be happy and your imagination to run wild, to create new ideas, to be a kid and grow up and enjoy your life. You've created a space where you can express yourself. You've made more time for yourself. You can now spend less time cleaning and more time being awesome, playing, and doing things you want to do.

You can use this extra time to get really good at something, start something new, make new friends, play with friends you already have, or whatever you want!

Bella has used a lot of her spare time to get better at drawing. In fact, she got so good at drawing and had so much more time in her days that she decided she wanted to start an online business where she sells her art and teaches other kids to draw. So she's started to create art courses for kids.

Leland has used most of his spare time to get super good at building LEGOs. Without any instructions or guidance, he builds creatures and animals just using LEGO pieces that he's collected over the years. He's been doing this for so long that he dreamed about how he can share this with others, and he's planning to start a YouTube channel to teach other kids how to build LEGO creations.

What do you want to use your extra time for?

_____

_____

_____

_____

Trying Something New

When you don't spend all your time cleaning your room or looking for items you've lost in your messy space or feeling tired from the heaviness that clutter creates, you can take the time to try new things.

Have you tried cooking and baking? Everyone loves to eat good food, and mastering a new recipe is such a great feeling!

What about gardening? Planting flowers, vegetables, or even trees is a great way to get creative, learn new things, and boost your mood (because being outside is good for our bodies!).

These kinds of activities are also a great way to give unique gifts! Give flowers to your grown-up, share cookies with friends, and make a whole meal for your family. You're learning and sharing some really cool stuff!

Look how far you've come in this process! **I am so proud of you!**

You have made positive changes, taken a look at your habits, cleaned and decluttered your space, and changed a piece of your life that will have an impact on all the other parts. This is huge!

One of the most important things you can do for yourself is celebrate your wins. Since you have accomplished so much, how do you want to celebrate? Even just having a new space to spend time in is a huge reward, but make sure you celebrate yourself beyond that. You deserve it!

Moving forward, remember what you've learned and how it felt to release clutter from your space and do things differently. This is a chance to live a different, lighter way than most people. Most people live their lives bogged down by stuff, but not you!

You're a boss now. The boss of your stuff.

aBout tHe autHoR

allie Casazza is on a mission to eradicate the "hot mess mom" stereotype by empowering other women. She has built a massive audience and a multimillion-dollar online business based on her proven, family-oriented approach to minimalism. She is the author of *Declutter Like a Mother*, the host of the chart-topping podcast *The Purpose Show*, and the creator of multiple online programs and courses that garner tens of thousands of registrations each time they run. Her platforms continue to grow every day as more women discover her life-changing approach to creating an abundant life. She lives in South Carolina with her husband, Brian, and her four children.